The College Volleyball Recruiting Playbook: Strategies for Success

A Comprehensive College Volleyball Recruitment Strategy Guide for Players & Parents

By John Forman

This book is dedicated to everyone looking to pursue the dream of playing volleyball in college, and to all those supporting them on that quest.

Preface

Welcome to The College Volleyball Recruiting Playbook: Strategies for Success. My name is John Forman, and I'm going to be your guide to getting recruited to play volleyball in college.

This is actually the second recruiting book I've worked on. The first I developed with a partner back in 2011. It was well-received, but has long since needed updating. A LOT has changed in the recruiting landscape since then!

This book provides that update in two ways. First, there's the obvious reflection of rules changes and other structural elements around recruiting. There was no Transfer Portal then. NIL wasn't a thing. Social media use was still in its relative infancy.

Second is my own significantly increased experience. I can now say that I've coached and recruited in all three NCAA divisions, plus at a university in the UK. I even coached a young international player who went on to play Division I volleyball in the US. All of this has allowed me to bring more breadth and depth of understanding to this book than to that prior one.

You'll notice, despite all that experience, this book isn't a particularly long read. That's because I wanted to come up with something tight and focused, with useful information on every page. No fluff.

Part I of the book covers the meat of the college recruiting process. That's the stuff basically everyone goes through. In contrast, Part II delves into more specialty situations – such as transfers and international recruitment – with a chapter dedicated to frequently asked questions. Plus, I've included an appendix sharing some ways you can use AI tools to help with the recruiting process.

My aim was for this to be a resource you can return to for specific, useful information and insights at all points along your recruiting journey. I think I've done that, and I hope you agree. If so, please post a review to let others know you found it helpful.

Now let's get to it!

Contents

Introduction

The journey from high school volleyball to college is thrilling, but it can also be daunting. This book aims to demystify the recruitment process. In doing so, it will provide you with the tools, knowledge, and confidence needed to make informed decisions about your future.

Recruiting is more than just showing off your athletic talent. It's about finding the right fit academically, athletically, and personally. It's about building relationships, showcasing your skills, and aligning your goals with those of potential college programs.

This book guides you through each step of this journey, from initial interest to signing day, and everything in between. We will cover eligibility essentials, the importance of academic performance, effective communication with college coaches, and strategies for leveraging your social media presence.

We'll also delve into the nuances of scholarship negotiations, the impact of official and unofficial visits, and the significance of understanding National Letters of Intent. Additionally, this guide provides insights into the unique challenges faced by interna-

1

tional recruits and transfer students, ensuring every prospective college volleyball player finds value in these pages.

This book is not just a collection of guidelines. It's a playbook tailored to the diverse paths of volleyball recruits. Every chapter addresses specific aspects of the recruiting process. Expert advice and practical tips infuse each chapter, supporting you at every turn.

The path to college volleyball is a journey of growth, resilience, and self-discovery. It will test your dedication and challenge your expectations. Ultimately, though, it will reward your hard work and passion for the game.

As you embark on this journey, remember that the goal is not just to play volleyball at the college level. It's enriching your life through the opportunities and experiences offered by both collegiate athletics and college life more broadly.

So, no matter whether you're aiming for the peak competition of NCAA Division I, the balanced experience of Division II or III, the unique opportunities within the NAIA, or the foundational start offered by Junior Colleges, this is your companion on the journey.

Let's dive in!

Part I

The College Recruiting Process

Chapter 1

College Volleyball vs. High School and Club

B efore we dive into all the recruiting stuff, let's take a moment to think about what it means to play volleyball in college. There's no doubt that playing in college differs from playing in high school or for a juniors club team. Just how different, though? Here are some ways.

Intensity of competition

For most, college volleyball represents a significant step up. You're playing with and against talented, experienced athletes from across the country, if not around the world. You'll almost invariably hear about the speed of the game if you ask current college players what the biggest difference is from high school or club. The players are more explosive and the tactics are more sophisticated. The learning curve is steep, for sure, but I think that's part of the excitement of making the jump to college.

Team dynamics

Being on a college team means integrating into a group of players from a variety of backgrounds. Chances are you will not know most (perhaps any) of your new teammates very well before you step on campus for your first year. Navigating this and adapting to a new team culture is a big part of making the move to college volleyball.

Schedules and demands

The daily schedule of a college student-athlete is demanding. You no doubt already have experience balancing practices, games, travel, and workouts with your academic responsibilities. College takes that to a new level. The pressure will always be on you to perform – on court and in the classroom. Learning to use the available resources effectively can make the difference in achieving both your academic and your athletic goals.

Coaching styles

You've no doubt had several coaches already in your playing career, so you know different coaches have different styles. That's true of college coaches as well. Some are very hands-on and detail-oriented, while others expect players to take more initiative. No matter what, though, college coaches will put greater demands on you than you've had before. This is something you'll have to embrace.

Bigger stage, brighter spotlight (potentially)

You may come from a school where volleyball enjoys a high profile and gets lots of people coming out to watch. No matter how much attention that brought, though, it pales compared to the attention that can come as a college athlete, depending on your level of play. This is an aspect of college sports that can be a lot of fun. After all, playing against your school's big rival in front of a packed gym of screaming home fans is an amazing experience. It also, however, requires maturity to handle. Fairly or unfairly, the expectations placed on student-athletes to uphold a higher standard of behavior both on and off the court are higher than for regular students. Missteps can have consequences, not just for you, but for your team and school.

Personal and professional growth

College sports offer many opportunities for personal and professional growth. No doubt you can easily come up with some of them off the top of your head, such as developing your athletic skills and building collaborative and leadership qualities. After all, volleyball has already allowed you to do those things. College, though, broadens that out. You'll be able to engage in networking and explore future career opportunities – be they in sports or elsewhere. These can have a major influence on your future.

Mental and physical health

The demands of being a student-athlete on your mental and physical health are significant. This can go both ways. Physically, you can develop your body in ways you may have never imagined, but of course, there is always the risk of injury. Mentally, being a student and athlete can help you develop tools to overcome life's challenges, but there will inevitably be times when you face overwhelm, confidence issues, and more. Fortunately, colleges typically provide access to a variety of resources to help you cope with the pressures and physical demands of student-athlete life.

Keep these differences in mind as we move forward from here to dive into the college volleyball recruiting process. The jump to college volleyball is not just a step up in competition; it's a whole new environment that offers both challenges and tremendous opportunity. Understanding that should underpin how you think about some decisions you need to make in your process.

Chapter 2

The Volleyball Recruiting Landscape

The shape of college volleyball – the organizations

V arious organizations and divisions govern the sport of college volleyball in the US and provide a structure for competition. Understanding the landscape of these organizations is essential for aspiring college volleyball players to navigate the recruiting process effectively.

By far the biggest of those, and the one most folks have heard about, is the NCAA - the National Collegiate Athletic Association. The National Association of Intercollegiate Athletics (NAIA) is an alternative to the NCAA among 4-year institutions, though significantly smaller (about 250 schools vs. about 1100).

There is also the National Christian College Athletic Association (NCCAA). As its name implies, the NCCAA brings together religious institutions. The membership is a little under 100, many of whom also hold membership in the NCAA or NAIA. The Association of Christian College Athletics (ACCA) is a similar group whose membership overlaps with the NCCAA.

For 2-year colleges (aka Junior Colleges or JUCOs), the National Junior College Athletic Association (NJCAA) is the leading organization, covering over 500 institutions, with the California Community College Athletic Association (CCCAA) overseeing schools in California. These can be good steppingstones into 4-year programs.

Underneath these top-level organizations, there are regional and conference affiliations. You no doubt have heard of the likes of the Big Ten, SEC, or ACC, which bring together schools with a set of commonalities. That could cover geography, academic standards, and size, among other things. These organizations set their own member rules on top of the national level ones (e.g., NCAA), though mostly they don't affect recruiting.

Comparing the Divisions

The NCAA operates three divisions: Division I, Division II, and Division III. Each division has its own characteristics and distinctions.

NCAA Division I is the most competitive level of college volleyball. It features the highest-profile programs, the top level of competition, and the greatest exposure. Division I schools typically have larger budgets, better facilities, and the most resources to support their volleyball programs. Athletes at this level have the greatest opportunities for full athletic scholarships, but possibly not as great as you think (see the next section).

Division II volleyball offers a slightly lower general level of competition compared to Division I, but still provides an exciting and competitive environment for student-athletes. Division II schools tend to have smaller enrollments and budgets. Athletic scholarships are available, but may be more limited in number and size. The aim of Division II programs is to offer a better balance between athletics and academics, providing student-athletes with opportunities to excel both on the court and in the classroom. This means a slightly shorter season than seen in Division I (except in Men's where Division II schools merge into Division I as a unified championship). Practically speaking, however, the two divisions are quite similar in their required time commitment and demands over the year.

Division III is where there is a strong emphasis on the student-athlete experience and integrating athletics within the overall educational journey. Athletes in Division III cannot receive athletic scholarships, as the focus is on pursuing academic excellence and personal growth. This translates into a shorter regular season and considerably reduced off-season training.

The NJCAA also operates a 3-division structure, with a similar type of breakdown. The NAIA, however, only has two divisions.

It is important to note **there's A LOT of overlap between the NCAA divisions** - as well as NAIA and NJCAA - in terms of level of play, resources, etc. For example, the upper-level Division II teams, and even Division III teams, would be very competitive in Division I. So would top NAIA and JUCO teams. As such, avoid thinking that Division I must be better than Division II, which is always better than Division III, that NCAA is necessarily better than NAIA, or that 4-year is better than JUCO. Yes, this is true if you're talking about the upper level of Division I. Below that, though, the situation is much more nuanced.

This is even more the case when considering athletic scholarships.

Athletic Scholarships – What you need to know

There are a lot of assumptions and misunderstandings out there about athletic scholarships. Frankly, there are also many people that mislead athletes about their prospects for getting a full athletic scholarship (a so called "full ride"). Let me explain the reality. I'm going to use the NCAA as the focus, as that's the reference point most people use.

As a starting point, I need to flag a major structural shift in Division I athletics aid that affects volleyball recruiting. Historically, indoor women's volleyball used a "headcount" model (a fixed number of full grants-in-aid), while men's volleyball and beach used an "equivalency" model (a pool of aid that could be split across athletes). Under the current Division I framework, the old scholarship-limit structure has largely been replaced by a roster-limit model, and athletics aid can be provided in any amount (full or partial), subject mainly to roster caps and each school's budget and priorities.

Under the current Division I model, roster limits (not scholarship counts) are the primary cap, and athletics aid can be provided in any amount (full or partial) to athletes within those roster limits. Practically, this means more players can receive athletics aid than before, but the amount and distribution will vary a lot by school and conference resources.

This is obviously a huge development as it opens up the potential for both a lot more scholarship money being available and a lot more players getting an athletic scholarship. The impact on the men's game, in particular, could be profound.

We need to keep something in mind, though.

Even before this, it was not the case that all Division I women's programs were fully funded. By that I mean they offered 12 full athletic scholarships. Yes, that is the case in the top conferences. At the other end, though, a lot of teams have had fewer than 12 to offer. And Ivy League schools don't offer any athletic scholarships at all (or academic ones either). While these new rules will expand the figures at the top end, lower down the impact on available scholarship is likely to be smaller, or even non-existent, though indoor women's teams will be able to have more than 12 players on scholarship now (this may seem like spreading the same amount of money over more players – which certainly could be the case – but there's some nuance around other aid coming from the school that factors in here).

The bottom line is that **there are far fewer full athletic scholarships available in Division I than most people likely believe**.

That may rise under the new rules, but the distribution of that increase is likely to be heavily weighted toward the top end of the sport.

Importantly, Division I volleyball is now constrained primarily by roster limits rather than a fixed number of scholarships. That can reduce roster sizes for programs that historically carried large squads. It will be interesting to see the impact that has moving forward. On the face of it, one would expect it to force players down the pyramid into Division II or III, or potentially into the NAIA – maybe even the JUCOs – because there are fewer total roster spots in Division I.

Turning to Division II, the scholarship limit for indoor women is 8. For the men it's 4.5. Beach teams get 5. At the time of publication there have been no indications of this changing, nor of roster limits being imposed. As with Division I, many programs in Division II are not fully funded.

And as noted above, there are no athletic scholarships in Division III. That doesn't mean there isn't institutional money, however. It would simply take the form of academic and/or other grants and scholarships. This is something very much worth keeping in mind as **you *could* end up with a better financial situation going to a Division III school than going Division I or II**, even if you receive an athletic scholarship. The same is true in terms of Division II vs. Division I.

NAIA schools operate more on an equivalency basis. Scholarship rules are more relaxed there than in the NCAA. Especially in Men's

Volleyball, you may find an NAIA school has more scholarship money available to offer, so don't ignore them.

Before moving on, it is important to note that currently a player on a beach scholarship may not compete for an indoor team under NCAA rules, but a player on an indoor scholarship may play for the school's beach team. I haven't seen any indication of this changing.

Don't Sleep on the JUCOs!

While most people reading this book are probably thinking mainly about being recruited to a 4-year college, don't ignore the 2-year college option. Here are some reasons a JUCO might be the better option for you.

- If you need to improve your grades or test scores to meet the eligibility requirements of a 4-year school. JUCOs often have smaller class sizes, allowing for more personalized attention and support from faculty, which can help with that.

- You can gain more playing experience and develop your skills at a JUCO, and also use it to attract attention from 4-year college coaches if you perform well, improving your chance of recruitment to a better program.

- JUCOs can be significantly less expensive than 4-year schools, reducing the financial burden and potentially minimizing student debt, and you might have better chances to earn athletic scholarships at a JUCO.

- If you're undecided on your major, you could start at a JUCO to explore different academic interests without the higher cost of a 4-year college.

- If you prefer to stay closer to home for personal reasons, a local JUCO can offer that option along with the opportunity to play volleyball.

When considering a JUCO, you'll want to consider how credits will transfer. The folks at the school should be able to talk you through that. If you have a specific target in mind for your eventual transfer, it's worth speaking to them as well.

It's worth also noting that good JUCO coaches can be a lot of help in moving you on to a 4-year school when you're done there. They understand that a big part of their job is helping student-athletes make that transition. As a result, they are often well-connected and will actively promote their players, which can come in very handy indeed.

See Chapter 14 for information about transferring from a JUCO to a 4-year school.

Comparing them all

Here's a table that compares the various organizations and levels.

Factor	NCAA Division I	NCAA Division II	NCAA Division III	NAIA	NJCAA
Scholarships	Full athletic scholarships available; largest scholarship budgets	Partial scholarships; mix of athletic and academic aid	No athletic scholarships; focus on academic and need-based aid	Athletic scholarships available; more flexibility in types of aid offered	Athletic scholarships available, often more limited in amount
Competition Level	Highest level of competition and visibility	High level of competition, but generally a lower level than Division I	Competitive but focuses more on balancing athletics with academics	Competitive level similar to NCAA Division II, with some variance	Can be quite competitive but typically a steppingstone to 4-year programs
Academic Programs	Wide range of academic programs, including many specialized fields	Wide range of academic programs, though slightly less variety than Division I	Strong emphasis on academics; range of programs depends on size	Good variety of academic programs; often focused on degrees and certificates; career readiness	Generally offers associate degrees and certificates; some specialized programs
Time Commitment	Very high; athletics often equated to a full-time job	High, but typically less demanding than Division I	Significant time commitment, but more balanced with academic pursuits	Similar to NCAA Division II	Moderate to high; depends on the program
Geographic Reach	Nationwide, with schools in nearly every state	Nationwide, but fewer schools than Division I	Nationwide, with a focus on smaller schools	Nationwide, with a strong presence in certain regions	Primarily local or regional
Facilities and Resources	State-of-the-art facilities and extensive support staff in many places	High-quality facilities, good support staff	Good facilities, but generally less extensive than Divisions I and II	Varies widely; some schools have excellent facilities, others more modest	Varies significantly; some schools have strong programs with good facilities
Recruiting Process	Highly competitive	Competitive; recruiting may start slightly later than Division I	Less intense; coaches often recruit later in high school	Competitive; recruiting process similar to NCAA Division II	Often recruits from local high schools and international students; more accessible
Post-Graduate Opportunities	Strong network of alumni, high visibility for professional opportunities	Good alumni network, solid professional opportunities	Strong focus on academics leads to good professional opportunities	Good alumni network; growing number of professional opportunities	Often a steppingstone to NCAA or NAIA programs, or professional opportunities in specific fields
Athlete Experience	High-profile, intense environment, significant media coverage	Competitive but with a more balanced college experience	Focus on holistic development, strong emphasis on student life	Balanced experience with competitive athletics and academic opportunities	Development-focused, preparing athletes for next-level opportunities

College Club Volleyball is an option too

I can't end this chapter without noting that not everyone who plays volleyball in college is part of the institutional ("varsity") team. There is also club volleyball, which is more student-run, and often operates through the campus recreation department. Sometimes – such as in Men's Volleyball – the school may not actually have a varsity team. Club is then the only option.

Club volleyball is not intramural. It's still inter-collegiate. Just at a lower level. There is, in fact, an entire organization overseeing it nationally: the National Collegiate Volleyball Federation (ncvf.or g). They even run national championships.

This can be a legitimate option for someone who wants to keep playing, but doesn't want the time commitment of being part of the regular team. Or if you really want to go to a certain school for the academics, but aren't at the level to be recruited to the regular team.

Chapter 3

NCAA Recruiting Terms and Rules

Since the NCAA is both the largest college sports organization and the one with the most intensive set of rules, it's worth taking some time to talk about those rules. There are some terms and key rules you should know going through the recruiting process. This isn't a complete list, but it should be helpful.

Please be aware that rules change. The ones mentioned here are accurate as of the time of publication. You can get a full set of rules for any of the divisions by searching "NCAA manual". Free PDF versions are available for download. Of course, if you're looking at an NAIA, NJCAA, or other type of school, I encourage you to check out their rules. Just know that if you're good under NCAA rules, you are almost certain to be good under the others.

Prospective Student Athlete (PSA): This is any athlete that has entered the 9th grade of high school, or someone younger who has received financial assistance or other benefits from an institution that aren't provided to normal prospective students. When someone becomes a PSA, NCAA recruiting rules kick in. (For international readers, US students graduate high school following 12th grade.)

NCAA Eligibility Center: The EC, which you may sometimes hear referred to as the Clearinghouse (its old name), is the system NCAA member schools used to verify the initial eligibility of incoming student-athletes. That covers both the academic and amateurism elements. Anyone planning to play at an NCAA institution must register with the EC, which the NCAA recommends you do at the start of your recruiting process. Do that at www.eligibilitycenter.org or https://web3.ncaa.org/ecwr3/. *Please note that there are different types of registration if you're going Division III rather than Division I or Division II, so pay attention and follow the instructions and guidance provided. The NAIA also has its own Eligibility Center (play.mynaia.org).*

First Permissible Contact Date: Division I rules prohibit any form of contact between college coaches and PSAs and/or their family members prior to June 15th at the end of the PSAs sophomore year (10th grade). This covers any form of contact, including calls, emails, and texts. There is no similar communication restriction for Divisions II or III, but Division II has the same limits on in-person contact as Division I. Note that Division I and II coaches can interact with players in a non-recruiting context prior to these dates at things like camps and clinics. They may not communicate about recruiting in those instances, however.

Quiet Period: This is a time during which recruiters may not take part in off-campus activity. Coaches can't go to events to scout players, or otherwise meet up with them away from campus, but PSAs can come to a campus on an Official or Unofficial Visit.

Dead Period: This is when no in-person activities can happen. That means no off-campus recruiting and no on-campus meetings, including Unofficial or Official visits. Even if the PSA is on campus for something else (e.g. an Open House), the volleyball staff cannot have face-to-face contact. *Note that this restriction does not apply once the PSA signs an NLI or makes a deposit following an offer of admission.*

Recruiting Calendar: The recruiting calendar includes the listing of all Contact (coaches allowed to have off-campus contact), Evaluation (coaches only allowed to watch, not have face-to-face contact), Quiet, and Dead Periods. It's good to know these to understand when and how college coaches can see you play and interact with you. If you search on "NCAA recruiting calendar" you should be able to find the dates for the current year. Note that there are different dates for Divisions I & II, and for Women's, Men's, and Beach. Division III doesn't have any date restrictions, so there really isn't a calendar.

Contact During Competition Events: NCAA rules for all divisions prohibit anything beyond incidental in-person contact (e.g. saying "Hi") on a competition day until the PSA's competition concludes for the day and their coach has released them. So if you're a PSA at a tournament, don't run up to a college coach during the day and try to talk to them. They cannot do so. This rule doesn't apply to parents, however, though keep the first permissible contact date in mind. Be aware that clubs and schools can have their own rules.

Unofficial Visit: This is a campus visit paid for by the PSA. The host institution may not cover any expenses in Division II and III, and it may only provide limited permissible items (for example, a small number of complimentary admissions to a home athletics event and, in some cases, a meal within the locale). A PSA can make an unlimited number of such visits. For Division I, visits can happen starting August 1st before the PSA's Junior year (11th grade). There are no restrictions in Division II and III.

Official Visit: The host institution pays for the cost of this visit - in part or fully. This includes travel to and from campus, meals, lodging, and admission to campus events. Also, the host institution can cover expenses for a limited number of family members who accompany the PSA. The visit can include up to two consecutive nights of lodging (timing details vary by division and circumstance). Normally, PSAs can only take one Official Visit to each host institution. The divisions have different dates for when a PSA can start doing Official Visits. They are August 1st and June 15th before Junior year for Divisions I and II respectively, and January 1st during Junior year for Division III.

Written Offer of Athletics Aid (replaces the NLI in Divisions I and II): Many schools now use a written offer/financial aid agreement process rather than the traditional National Letter of Intent structure. These documents outline the athletics aid being offered and the conditions attached to it; the exact form and effects can vary by school, conference, and division. Signing windows are sport-specific and can change, so confirm the current signing rules and dates for your division and target schools.

Qualifier/Partial Qualifier/Non-Qualifier: These are NCAA designations for incoming student-athletes regarding their academic standing. A Qualifier is someone who meets all required academic standards for initial eligibility. A Partial Qualifier (used only in Division II) is someone who meets some, but not all, of the academic requirements. They can do most things, but they may not compete during their first year at the school. A Non-Qualifier doesn't meet the NCAA's required academic standards. They cannot take part in any athletically related activities in their first year, nor can they receive athletic scholarship funding.

Verbal (Unofficial) Offer: A verbal offer is any offer of an athletic scholarship made by a coach to a PSA prior to issuing an NLI. This can happen any time from the first permissible contact date onwards. Offers only become official when you get an NLI.

Walk-On: We commonly refer to a college player not on an athletic scholarship at a Division I or II school as a walk-on. Some walk-ons are athletes who started attending a school, then later joined the volleyball team – perhaps through a tryout. These days, most teams recruit walk-ons. This means that the team recruits them to join the team, but they do not receive an athletic scholarship - at least not when they first arrive. Walk-ons can sometimes receive a scholarship later.

Chapter 4

The Recruiting Timeline

In this chapter, I'm going to outline the basic timeline recruits go through. Then I'll present a kind of ideal progression. Of course, everyone will have their own specific timeline based on their circumstance.

The General Progression

Broadly speaking, a recruiting timeline is going to look something like this:

1. Decide you want to play volleyball in college

2. Come up with at least some idea of where you'd like to go to school

3. Develop your recruiting materials

4. Reach out to places you'd like to be recruited, respond to schools reaching out to you, and engage in communication

5. Visit schools

6. Field offers

7. Decide

Some of the first few steps could happen in a different order, or happen in a more intertwined fashion. For example, you might have some schools in mind from an academic perspective, then decide to pursue college volleyball. And some of those steps could be ongoing (thinking about where you want to go, developing your recruiting materials). One way or another, though, the recruiting process includes these steps.

In future chapters, I'll address all of them – except the deciding to play part. You probably already have that covered if you're reading this book.

The Ideal Timeline

Here's what an ideal timeline for recruiting would look like.

Freshman Year (and earlier)
- **Focus on:** Skills, Physical Development, Academics, Enjoying the Sport
- **Recruiting Notes:** Division I and II coaches cannot communicate with you. Likely too early for Division III, NAIA, and JUCO coaches. Watch college volleyball to understand the game at different levels.

Sophomore Year
- **Focus on:** Keep working on physical and technical development
- **Recruiting Notes:** Still early for Division III, NAIA, and JUCO coaches. For Division I and II prospects: Develop your recruiting profile, create and share video highlights, develop a list of target schools and initiate communication, consider Unofficial Visits if permissible.

Junior Year
- **Focus on:** Full speed ahead on recruiting. Sustain communication with target schools. Making adjustments to target list. Keep doing well in the classroom.
- **Recruiting Notes:** Develop a decision timeframe. Make Official and Unofficial visits. Accept verbal offers if within your decision timeframe.

Senior Year
- **Focus on:** Finalize your college decision. Finish the job academically. Enjoy your last year of high school.
- **Recruiting Notes:** If you've accepted a Verbal Offer, sign your NLI in November (or thereafter). If not, continue communication and visits until you finalize your decision.

Freshman Year (9th grade): Focus on improving your skills, working on your physical development (with proper medical/professional guidance), getting good grades, and having fun. Division I and II coaches can't communicate with you. Honestly, unless you are among maybe the top 0.5%, they're probably not even looking this early. It's also likely too early for Division III, NAIA, and JUCO coaches to be thinking about players in your year. So don't focus much on recruiting. It's a good idea to watch a bunch of college volleyball, though. Doing so will give you a sense of what the game looks like at different levels, which will be useful later. It'll also give you a sense of how you can develop your own game.

Sophomore Year (10th grade): This is still probably early for most Division III, NAIA, and JUCO coaches, so if you're thinking about something in that area, you can continue to relax and focus on getting better and enjoying your volleyball. And continuing to do well in school, of course. For Division I and II prospects, though, the club season will be time to put some work in. You'll want to develop your recruiting profile, or at least put together some video to share. Develop a list of target schools and initiate communication with them. They won't be able to respond until later, but at least you'll get on their list for evaluation. Look at doing college visits as your calendar permits – making them Unofficial Visits if permissible.

Junior Year (11th grade): Full speed ahead, no matter which level you're targeting. Develop a sense of when you would like to have a decision in place. Sustain communication with your target schools - making adjustments along the way. Make Official Visits where available, and Unofficial Visits where it makes sense. If it's in your decision timeframe and you get a Verbal Offer, you are welcome to accept.

Senior Year (12th grade): If you've accepted a Verbal Offer, sign your NLI when the time comes in November (or thereafter) and enjoy your last year of high school! Otherwise, continue what you've been doing until you have a final decision in place.

Make Your Own Timeline

As I said, the timeline above is idealized. People come into it at all different points along the way, and with an array of considerations. Some make a late decision to play college volleyball, so have to play catch-up. Some have very specific academic desires, so can operate in a very concentrated fashion from that perspective, while others let the volleyball lead the way (I'll speak more to this later).

The point is, ultimately, everyone has their own recruiting timeline driven by their own particular situation. No need to panic if things don't look exactly like what you see above. Lots of athletes who don't go through the process this way get recruited every year. The rest of the book will help you navigate that, no matter what that is for you.

A Note on Your Academics

The stronger your transcript and test scores (if applicable) the more options you create for yourself. Not only does it bring more schools into frame for you, it also increases the potential amount of academic aid you may get in the form of scholarships and/or grants. Plus, college coaches like players who will do well in class and not cause them academic headaches. So don't just focus on the volleyball!

Chapter 5

Creating Your Target List of Schools

N ow we get to a subject I harp on relentlessly with those going through the recruiting process. That's thinking about what you want as you plan what schools to target. Picking a college is a big decision. There are lots of factors involved in it you should at least consider. In this chapter, I'm going to take you through them.

We'll start with the two top-level considerations. Those are the academic and athletic pieces.

Academic criteria

At the most basic level, you want to create a list of schools with the major(s) you have in mind. For some majors, like biology, there are tons of schools with that option. In other cases, like engineering, the list is shorter. And if you're aiming for something quite specialized, such as underwater archaeology, the list of schools will be quite short.

You also want a school that will be the right level of challenge for you. If you're an upper level student in high school, for example, you probably wouldn't find most JUCOs academically challenging. Similarly, if you're only a mediocre high school student, the likes of Stanford or the Ivy League schools would probably be aiming too high. I think a good list consists mainly of schools that you consider being at the right academic level, with a few stretch ones and a few fallbacks mixed in as well. If you have a good guidance counselor at your high school, they should be able to help you with this kind of targeting.

Note that you should look at these things in combination, and not just think of them as separate. There are well-respected universities that aren't very strong in one or more majors. There are also schools that don't rank all that highly but which have an outstanding department for a certain major. So if the academic piece is important to you, and you have a good sense of what you want to study, you'll want to go that little bit deeper in your research.

Not sure what you want to study in college? That's fine. A lot of recruits are in that situation, especially in the earlier stages of the process. Some don't really decide until they get there. Plus, lots of people change to something different during college. If you're unsure right now, it's worth considering the breadth of options each school offers. That way, you'll have a better chance of there being what you want without having to transfer (we deal with transferring later).

Athletic Criteria

In terms of the broad athletic consideration, what we're mainly talking about here is the level of play. There is a tendency to think in terms of NCAA Division here, but as I pointed out in Chapter 2, there's a lot of overlap across divisions. And there's a big spread within divisions as well. The Big Ten is on a whole different level than The Big South, for example. And even within conferences, there can be significant differences.

I mentioned in the last chapter how it can be very useful to watch a lot of college volleyball from a variety of levels. This is where that helps. You want to be realistic when developing your list of target schools from an athletic perspective, just as you do from an academic one.

Compare yourself physically and technically to players in your position – especially current 1st year players if you can. And if you hear about players who are at or near the same level as you committing to schools, that's probably a pretty good sign of the level you want to target. Your coach(es) should be able to help with this. And if you're at a club with a recruiting coordinator, they should be able to as well.

Environment – The School

After considering the overall academic and athletic aspects, you can then narrow down your list based on other factors. In particular, you need to think about the environment you want to be in at school.

While the volleyball part of your life at college will be important, you will spend more time immersed in the rest of the campus atmosphere between going to classes, spending time with friends, living in campus housing, etc. As such, you want to consider what kind of environment you want to be in.

Here's a list of considerations, in no particular order.

- Size of campus

- Student population

- Urban vs. Sub-urban vs. Rural

- Climate and Geography

- Distance from home (or other desired location)

- Campus aesthetic (does liking how it looks matter?)

- Cultural and social atmosphere

- Diversity

- Safety and security

- Health services (including mental health and well-being)

- Residential life (dorms, etc.)

- Dining and other food options

- Campus facilities

- Student activities

Some of these will certainly matter more to you than others. You may not realize how you actually rank things, though, until you get on campus and see things for yourself. That's why it can be very useful to go on visits. Even visits to schools you may not really be considering can be helpful because they give you a chance to see distinct elements.

Environment – The Volleyball

Now let's consider the volleyball environment. Here too there are several factors you'll want to examine and think about.

- **Historical performance:** If being in a winning team matters to you, then you'll want to see how a team has done in recent years. That's not a guarantee of how they'll do in the future, but it's at least an indication. And be sure to look at how the other teams at the school perform as well. If they are mostly doing well, then you're probably looking at a competitive athletic department. If they're mostly low down in the standings, then there's a good chance the department lacks the resources of others in their league.

- **Coaching staff tenure:** How long has the head coach been there? Someone who's been there for a while may be more likely to stay than someone only there a short time. And programs with newer head coaches are often going through significant changes. If stability matters to you, this is something to look at. Since assistant coaches move more frequently, I wouldn't worry too much about them having short tenures, unless there's a pattern of assistants only staying a year or two. That could be a red flag.

- **Who's playing most?**: A program which features upper-classmen as its starters (not counting transfers) is likely to be one where player development is a feature. If, however, it's regularly underclassmen and/or transfers getting lots of playing time, then that might be a situation where the staff is looking to recruit better players rather than developing those they have.

- **Transfer frequency:** If you see a lot of players transferring out of the program, that's definitely a warning sign. I'm not talking so much about the case of a new coaching staff, but if you see a pattern over a few years, something might not be right.

- **Facilities:** What are the practice, competition, and other facilities like, especially compared to schools at a similar level?

- **Support staff:** How do things like academic support (advisors, tutors, study hall, class scheduling) and trainer/medical coverage compare to similar schools?

- **Team academics:** Not all schools list them (though you can ask), but seeing what players on the team are studying and how they're doing can say a lot about how academically minded the players are, what areas of study fit well with being an athlete, and things like that.

Because the focus of this chapter is on building your target list, I've left some things out here that will come into play later. Mainly, I've tried to focus on things you can evaluate by looking at the school's website. We'll cover other topics like coaching style and team dynamics later.

Managing your list

The length of your target list ultimately depends on the strength of your preferences and the narrowness of your focus. Go too narrow and you could really limit your options. Go too broad and your list may be quite long. You want to find the balance between giving yourself enough opportunities to be recruited while not making managing it all overwhelming.

And don't feel like your target list has to be etched in stone. Use what you learn along the way to refine it. I've mentioned a bunch of environmental considerations in this chapter, any of which you may change your mind about. Similarly, you could change your intended area of study during the process. That's fine. It's part of the broader college process and experience – learning about yourself.

Chapter 6

Developing Your Recruiting Materials

N ow let's talk about what you should have in terms of recruiting materials. There are two main things you need – a profile and video. I'll address each of them in this chapter.

Your recruiting profile

A recruiting profile is basically all the information about you a college coach might want to develop at least a preliminary idea of who you are and what you bring to the table. This includes:

- **Photo:** So coaches can put a face to a name, which can be very helpful when trying to pick you out while watching you play or meeting you.

- **Name:** Schools will eventually need it, so provide your legal name. If that doesn't match what's on your team's rosters, make sure you include that as well (e.g. Lizzy vs.

Elizabeth).

- **Address:** At this point you don't need to list your full home address, but city and state (and country, if outside the US) should be there.

- **Contact Info:** At a minimum, list an email address. While coaches would prefer your regular email, it's fine to use one that's strictly for recruiting communication here. If you want, you can list your phone number as well, or you can hold that back until you have actual communication with a school.

- **High School (or equivalent)**

- **Club Team (if you have one)**

- **Graduation Year**

- **Height**

- **Position(s)**

- **Jump Reach (if you have it):** Preferably both approach and blocking. Obviously unnecessary for a libero/DS. And if you're a setter, it's the blocking number that matters. Don't fudge this number. Coaches will be able to tell pretty quickly once they see you play.

- **GPA:** Note the scale if it's not based on a 4.0.

- **Test Scores:** Many schools don't require them, but if

you've taken the SAT and/or ACT, and have a score you're good with, post that.

- **Intended College Major:** If you know it, or have some ideas, list it (or them). If not, you can just put Undecided. It's fine not to know when you're early in your process. By senior year, though, you should have at least narrowed things down somewhat (though some people do start college undecided)

- **Personal Statement:** This isn't strictly necessary, but it can be quite good to have. It gives recruiters a chance to learn more about you, is a way you can highlight things that might make you stand out, and is potentially an opportunity for you to explain any negative issues if there were mitigating circumstances.

- **Video:** Depending on how you put your profile together, you may include an uploaded video or links (more coming on this).

- **Current Schedule:** You don't need to include this, but it can be useful for coaches when they're planning their recruiting travel. If it's not on your profile, they'll potentially ask you for it, so make sure it's at least quickly available for you to share.

There are a couple of different ways you can put your profile together. Probably the most popular these days is via one of the recruiting services (I talk about these in the FAQ chapter). Many of them allow you to create a free profile on their system. This can be very convenient in that all you need to do is provide people with a link. And you can update things easily. Plus, your profile is searchable by college coaches.

The other way to go is to create some kind of profile document – like a PDF. You can then send that out to coaches. If you want to see examples of this, do an image search on "sample volleyball recruiting profile". When I did that I saw several examples from Pinterest.

Whichever way you go, if you're under 18, you need to make sure you have parental/guardian permission to share your personal information.

Video

Now on to one of the biggest pieces of the recruiting process – your video. You probably want two primary videos. One is a highlight reel. That's a quick introduction to you as a player. It's intended to attract attention. Here are my recommendations for putting that together.

- **Camera:** A phone or tablet camera is of more than sufficient quality. Be sure to use landscape mode, though.

- **Introduction:** Put some kind of identifying info at the beginning of your video. Name, position, and graduation year are the minimum. If you want to show off your personality a bit, you can record a personal message, but that's definitely not mandatory. Obviously, be cautious about what you include in something that is public.

- **Viewing angle:** The end line view is the one preferred. It's the angle coaches use when they're scouting other teams, so they're used to judging things this way. I know a lot of schools stream their matches using mid-court cameras, and it's really easy to just take that video. If you can, though, you're better off having someone record from behind the court. If you're a hitter or setter, avoid high angle mid-court sideline views. From this angle, it's hard for coaches to get a sense of how high hitters and blockers get and set quality. It's fine for showing court movement, though. Here are examples of end line and mid-court views:

Best to use this angle.

Avoid this angle, if you can.

- **Make sure they can pick you out:** There's nothing more frustrating to a coach than not being able to figure out who they're supposed to be looking at. Some people use things like pointers in the video to indicate themselves. That's useful – if you don't get too crazy with it. Another option is to put your number at the beginning of the video (and at any time it might change) and say which side you're on. Basically, think about how you can point yourself out to someone who's never seen you before and do that.

- **Stick to the best stuff:** Be selective in what you include. Only use the best of the best in your video.

- **How long?:** Aim for 2-3 minutes, 5 minutes tops. If you're a 6-rotation player, you'll probably be on the longer end than a front row or back row only player, but you still want to keep it tight and focused. Recruiters don't need to see 50 reps. They'll be fine with 10 if those are the right reps. If they want to see more, they will ask.

- **Structure:** Probably the most common structure for recruiting videos is to have separate sections (preferably labeled somehow) for each skill you want to present. This is a good way to go.

- **What to include:** Put in stuff that really shows off your skill and physical capabilities, even if the play didn't work out in your favor. And make sure you cover all the skills of your position in your video. Recruiters want to see the full set. Don't be that 6-rotation OH who doesn't show any passing or defense footage. That just makes the coach wonder about your ball-handling. Same with a setter who only shows their setting. What about defense and blocking?

- **What to exclude:** Overpass kills. Plays that are more about someone else being bad than you being good (like blocking someone trying to hit a poor set). Anything more than a handful of serves. A bunch of tips and/or off-speed hits (a couple of smart ones are fine to show that's in your toolkit).

- **Substance over flash:** This applies mainly to passing and defense. There is a tendency to include "exciting" plays, but that's not what recruiters care about. In fact, it can be counterproductive. For ball-handling, coaches are assessing things like anticipation, movement, and technique. If your video is just clips of you diving around, it can bring up questions about whether you're hitting the floor all the time because you're not positioned properly. A couple of these clips are fine, but make sure the focus is on demonstrating your skill set.

- **For setters:** It doesn't have to be a kill to be an excellent set. And flipping that around, just because it's a kill, doesn't make up for a poor set. Concentrate on showing off your accuracy, tempo, and decision-making.

- **No pauses in play:** I've seen many videos where people pause in the middle of something like an approach to highlight the player in focus. That's great from an identification perspective, but it impairs the coach's ability to gauge the player's explosiveness, quickness, and things like that. If you need to use a pause for identification, or some other reason, put it in before the action (e.g. the approach) starts.

- **Slow motion and replay:** Leave these out. If a coach wants to see a play again, they can rewind the video. And just as with pausing in the middle of a play, slow motion takes away the coach's ability to judge explosiveness, etc. If you want to use one bit of slow-motion (or pause) to show something like how high you reached on that hit or block, that's fine. Just don't do it repeatedly. I've seen highlight reels where the second half is just everything from the first half replayed in slow motion. I never watched that part. It was useless for my purposes.

- **Hudl highlights:** DO NOT simply grab your Hudl highlights and make that your recruiting video. A lot of time, those highlight reels include stuff coaches don't want to see (see above). Use only the best stuff.

- **Put your best stuff first:** You want to grab attention as quickly as possible at the beginning of your reel. If you put your best clip(s) at the beginning – even if it doesn't fit in with the rest of the video's structure – it will motivate coaches to keep watching, which is what you want.

The other video you'll want is full match footage. A lot of coaches will ask you for that after seeing your highlights. It gives them a chance to see how you move around the court, interact with teammates, etc. You don't need to include it in your profile, but it's good to have on-hand to provide upon request.

Now let me offer some additional tips on that match video beyond what I already mentioned for highlight videos.

- **Which match?** Pick the highest level of play you can, and the most competitive match possible. Don't pick something lopsided or played at a low level. Recruiters won't get much out of them. Of course, it should also be a match you played well in. So if you have a video of you playing really well in a tightly contested match against your big rivals, use that.

- **Edits:** While college coaches want full match video to see the broad scope of your game, they appreciate you saving them time with some judicious editing. You can leave out any time you're not on the court. And if you can also trim or fast forward through the breaks between points, even better!

- **Hudl links:** Chances are you won't just be able to share a school or club match video from Hudl with a college coach. They won't have permission to see it. Instead, get a download of the match video and upload it some place like YouTube. Then you can share it from there.

Before I wrap up, I want to say something about **individual clips**. Those are for social media where people just see one clip and watch that. If you have something really special that you want to show off, fine. Include that in your recruiting profile. Don't include a lot of individual clips there, though. It takes time for coaches to go through each one individually – time they're probably not going to take. That's why you do a highlight reel. If you present them separately, you might appear as someone too lazy to put them all together into one video.

University Athlete

If you play in the sort of Juniors tournaments in the US that attract college coaches (think national and larger regional events), make sure you're on University Athlete. This is the system coaches use at tournaments to know who's playing where and when. They also use it to make notes and keep rankings and ratings. For many schools, it's a cornerstone of how they track recruits.

In most situations, it's your club that does the bulk of the work ensuring that all the correct information on team rosters is in University Athlete. That's things like player number, position, etc.

You'll want to make sure you know what's on the system, though. First, you need to confirm that everything is correct. Second, you can add additional information (school, grades, video, etc.). It's not as full-on a profile as you might otherwise create elsewhere, but it's not massively far off either.

And schools sometimes use University Athlete as a recruit search platform. So you want to be on there with the right info.

Chapter 7

Your Social Media Platform

E ffectively utilized, social media can significantly enhance your visibility and attractiveness to college volleyball programs. Poorly utilized, social media can be a major detriment.

By maintaining a positive online presence, sharing your athletic and academic journey, and engaging responsibly with content, you can leverage social media as a powerful tool in your recruitment arsenal and beyond. While there isn't the scope here for a thorough analysis of effectively using social media, I will offer here some key points of focus.

Understanding Social Media's Role

Social media allows recruits to create a positive and compelling online presence, serving as an extension of your recruiting profile. It can offer a more dynamic and personal glimpse into your athletic abilities, work ethic, and personality. To do that, you'll want to create a positive online presence by:

- **Having Profile Consistency**: Your social media presence should reflect the same information as your recruiting materials. Use your real name and include details like your position, graduation year, and team.

- **Highlighting Your Athletic Achievements**: Share updates about your volleyball journey, including awards, personal milestones, game highlights, and training progress. Tag your school and club teams to increase visibility.

- **Don't Forget the Other Elements**: Remember that recruiters aren't just looking at you for your volleyball skills. They're also interested in what you're like as a student and a person. Post content that supports the picture of you that you want college coaches and future teammates to see.

- **Engaging Responsibly**: Follow and respectfully interact with college volleyball programs, coaches, and current players. All likes, comments, and shares should be positive and appropriate.

Content Dos and Don'ts

It's really easy to get tripped up on social media and do something that causes college coaches to look elsewhere. There are all kinds of stories out there about recruits who posted something stupid and had an offer pulled. Do a search online and you'll see plenty of examples. Colleges don't want that kind of thing associated with their brand. With that in mind, here are some dos and don'ts for what you post and share.

- **Do Share Team Successes**: Celebrate your team's achievements and showcase your role in those successes. Volleyball is a team sport, and this shows your ability to be a team player.

- **Do Post Training and Workout Videos**: Videos of training sessions, workouts, or skill drills can highlight your dedication and improvement. As such, they are suitable supporting material for what recruiters see in your highlight video, recruiting profile, communications, etc.

- **Don't Share Negative Content**: Avoid posting or sharing content that people could view as negative. Definitely don't post criticism of coaches, teammates, and/or officials!

- **Do be Regular and Consistent**: If you only post sporadically, you probably won't get people following you.

- **Don't Overlook Privacy Settings**: Regularly review your privacy settings to manage who can see your posts. But also remember that nothing online is truly private.

- **Do Think Before You Post**: Any time you're thinking about posting or sharing something – or even liking or commenting – consider whether that supports the image you're creating. This isn't just about recruiting. It might also play into other opportunities (see the NIL chapter).

- **Do Engage the Broader Volleyball Community**: Social media is a powerful networking tool. Engaging with the broader volleyball community – including both your peers and the likes of pro and college players and coaches – can both broaden your recruiting exposure and potentially grow your platform for other purposes.

Note that your online presence extends beyond social media. You should regularly search your name online to see what comes up. If there's any content that might negatively affect your recruitment prospects – or your public profile – then you'll want to address it.

Communication with Coaches

There are a couple of things to keep in mind when thinking of using social media to communicate with coaches. First, the rules for NCAA Division I and II coaches restrict direct messaging between them and recruits until a certain point in the recruiting process (see Chapter 3). That's assuming a coach even uses social media for communication (many don't). So you won't want to rely on that (more on this in the next chapter).

That doesn't mean they can't view your social media profile(s), however. You can use this as an indirect channel of communication, both with recruiters and potential future teammates.

How so?

By doing things like posting about your visits to their colleges or participation in their volleyball camps. By talking about their latest match or a newsworthy development (All-Conference selections, academic awards, etc.).

Of course, most of these sorts of updates and posts involve tagging the school's volleyball program account. How effective that is depends on who manages the account. If it's the coaching staff, perfect! If it's someone in Sports Information, tagging will not bring attention to you in the same way. Still worth doing, though!

Chapter 8

Reaching Out to College Coaches

D o not expect college coaches to come to you. It happens, but you don't want to rely on it. You are much more likely to end up in the right situation if you take charge of your recruiting process. This chapter will focus on how to start this process with the first email.

Just a quick reminder, though, to make sure you know where you are in the cycle. Remember from Chapter 3 that there are different rules depending on your age and the coaches you're targeting.

Questionnaires

Before we get on to emailing coaches, we should address questionnaires. Most schools have them in some fashion. How much coaches use them varies widely, however. Some use them extensively, others barely at all. Filling out a school's recruiting questionnaire is definitely a way to get on their list, but I would strongly recommend following up with an email. That way, if that coach doesn't really look at the questionnaires, you still get your information in front of them.

Getting contact information

I can just about guarantee that you'll find contact information for the volleyball coaches on the school website. Usually, the athletics website is separate from the main one for the school. It's easy to find, though. Just search for something like "Radford volleyball" and you'll get there. Then either look for the volleyball roster or coaches' page, or find the general staff directory and you'll get what you need.

Quick note: Follow any specific instructions you might see about recruiting contact. For example, some schools want you to email the "volleyball@" account. If you see that kind of thing, don't ignore it and blast the entire coaching staff. You'll just cause more work, which is not the first impression you want to make.

Sending from your own account preferred

College coaches prefer to get emails from the recruits themselves, not from a parent account. Of course, they expect patents to be involved in things, but it should be the recruit driving the process. So no parental emails as introductions. They are definitely marks against.

Also, be cautious about sending emails via a recruiting platform. Some coaches simply won't look at emails that come from services. In other cases, there can be systemic blocks, so coaches never actually get the emails. I'm not saying this is true in every, or even most, cases. It's just something to be aware of, especially if you're not getting a response.

Email subject line

The job of an email subject line is to get the person to open the email. In recruiting, though, there's a second purpose. That's classification. Recruiters get A LOT of email across multiple recruiting classes and positions. It's really useful to them to know what they're looking at when something hits the inbox. Those emails are likely to get looked at first – frankly, because it's just easier for them.

There's a very simple formula for the subject line of your initial email. If your name isn't clear from your email's "From" (if you're not sure, email someone and check), or you're using someone else's email (like a parent's), start with that. Then put your high school graduation year, your height, and your position. For example, "2025 6' OH". That's your bare minimum.

Now, maybe this is enough to get your email opened, but a little extra info can increase the odds. Think about what would make you stand out. Do you have a 40" vertical jump? Are you #1 in your class? Is there something about you that really fits with that school and/or team? Include that in your subject line. Just don't put too much. Remember, they will only see a limited number of characters, especially if they're on their phone.

Email body

The #1 job of the body of the email is to get the coach to watch your highlight video, which we talked about in Chapter 6. Fortunately, if you get them to open the email, the job is nearly done. All you have to do is make sure the link to your video (much preferred over an attachment) is very obvious.

It will probably only be after they watch your video that they read the rest of the email. Essentially, what they're doing is evaluating the volleyball side of things, then looking to see if the rest of it supports.

As for what's in the rest of the email body, if you aren't sending them to your online profile to watch your highlight video, you'll want to share that. The profile is often the next thing a recruiter will jump too because of all the info it provides in a well-structured format.

From there, it's about highlighting and connecting. Highlight key stuff from your profile that makes you stand out – and specifically stand out in regard to that school/team – some of which you may have included in your subject line (which you should reinforce). Connect by showing off your knowledge about the program and give them a sense of your fit with them.

Don't go too far with this, though. A paragraph or two will suffice. Chances are, much more than that will get skimmed at most. Unless you make a REALLY bad impression, it's unlikely a recruiter is going to decide on you as a person in the first email. You're just showing them you're interested and why they should be interested in you. Deeper stuff will come on calls, visits, etc.

Sample initial email

Here's a sample template for what your initial email could look like. Note that it's the sort that would be sent during the college team's season.

Subject: 2025 5'10" Lefty All-State Setter, 3.6 GPA
Email Body:
Dear Coach [Last Name],

My name is [Your Full Name], and I am a 5'10" left-handed [Your Position, e.g., Setter] from [Your High School] in [City, State]. I am currently a [Your Grade, e.g., Junior] and play club volleyball for [Your Club Team Name]. I have been following the [School Name] volleyball program and am very interested in the opportunity to be a part of your team.

I have been impressed by your team's recent success, particularly [mention a specific game, tournament, or achievement], and I admire your coaching style and philosophy. I believe that my skills and dedication would be a great fit for your program.

Here are a few highlights of my volleyball career so far:

Achievements: [List notable achievements, e.g., "Captain of the high school varsity team for two years," "MVP of the regional tournament," "Selected for the All-State team"]

I have linked my highlight video below to give you a better sense of my playing style and abilities.

Academic Performance: [Include GPA and any academic honors, e.g., "Current GPA: 3.8," "Member of the National Honor Society"]

I am very interested in [School Name] because of its strong academic programs, particularly in [Your Intended Major], and the opportunity to contribute to a competitive and dynamic volleyball program. I would love to learn more about your team and discuss how I can be a part of [School Name] volleyball.

Thank you very much for your time and consideration. I look forward to the possibility of speaking with you soon.

Best regards,

[Your Full Name]

[Your Phone Number]
[Link to Highlight Video]

Please note that I'm not suggesting you use this exact template. You want something that is specific to you. So adjust it and adapt it to reflect who you are and what you bring to the table. Or get AI to help you come up with one for you (see the Bonus chapter).

Initial email fails

There are two big ways introductory recruiting emails to coaches fail. Top of the list is not sharing video. That can either be forgetting to include a link to it, or including a link that doesn't work. So be sure that you always have a link to your latest highlight video in your emails and that the link goes where you want it to go. Test that! Send it to a friend to make sure it works.

The other big fail is not doing your research. I can't tell you how many times I got emails from prospective recruits who clearly hadn't checked things out. The most frequent example is saying you're interested in an academic major the school doesn't have. This sort of basic mistake doesn't impress recruiters.

Oh, and I should also mention clear cut-and-paste emails. Coaches get it that recruits are reaching out to multiple schools, so they're forgiving here. Just don't make it really obvious. Each school wants to feel sought after in its own right, after all.

Texting or social media for first contact

I specifically talked in this chapter about doing initial contact via email for a reason. Email is very easy for college coaches to sort, file, etc. It also often integrates with the systems they use to manage their prospect lists. Given that you may reach out to them when they're not allowed to respond (per Chapter 3), or during part of the year when they have little time (like the middle of season), an initial contact via email is easy to refer back to at a later date. Texts and DMs are less easy to manage that way.

Of course, there's also the question of access. It's easy to get email addresses since they're posted publicly. A lot of coaches, however, don't have their mobile phone numbers listed. And many coaches don't use social media at all for recruiting beyond making sure you aren't posting stuff that would exclude you from consideration.

Chapter 9

Navigating Communication After Initial Contact

After initial contact, you need to further that communication based on the response you get. In this chapter, I'll provide strategies for managing that ongoing communication. Be aware that in many cases it will be an assistant coach rather than the head coach that does most recruiting communication. Don't take that as a negative.

The Recruit Talks Most

Before I get into the finer points of communication and contact after the initial phase, I need to address parental involvement. It is VERY IMPORTANT that the recruit is the center of attention – particularly for any kind of face-to-face interaction and/or call.

It is totally fine – and fully expected – that parents have questions. The recruit, however, must be the one doing most of the talking. Coaches use these interactions to learn more about the recruit's personality – and frankly how much of a pain the parent(s) might be. If a parent dominates the conversation, then red flags go up in the coach's mind. You don't want that.

Responding to Coaches' Feedback

After your initial outreach, there are three main things that will happen. Here's how to handle each:

Positive Response: Express gratitude and interest in learning more about their program. Ask specific questions about things that matter to you in the decision-making process (about the team, academic support, etc.) and next steps in the recruiting process.

Neutral Response: If the response is non-committal, thank them for the reply and express continued interest. Provide updates as appropriate (see below).

No Response or Negative Feedback: If feedback is explicitly negative, thank them for their consideration and turn your attention elsewhere. If you don't get a reply, don't become immediately concerned. It could simply be a timing issue. Follow-up in a few weeks. If you've emailed multiple times and have heard nothing back (assuming they are allowed to reply per the rules) then it's a sign you should scratch that school from your list.

Ongoing Communication

It's important to stay in regular contact with any school from which you've had a positive – or at least non-negative - response. This lets them know you remain interested, which can be very important when recruiting timelines can cover multiple years. It also allows you to gather further information for your own decision-making when that time comes.

Here are the ways you can keep the lines of communication open.

- **Regular Updates**: Keep the coaches informed of your academic and athletic progress. Highlight recent achievements, awards, and the like. In other words, reinforce why you make a strong prospect for their program. Make sure you customize your updates to each coach and/or program, especially if you can tie what you've been doing specifically to something related to that school or volleyball team.

- **New Video**: If you have an updated highlight reel, send it. Just make sure it's not stuff they've already seen. And if you had a fantastic match recently, share the link to that. What they most want to see is your continued development, so feature that as much as you can.

- **Show Engagement**: Let the coaches know you're paying attention to what's going on in the program by reaching out about their recent developments. That could be checking in about their latest match, offering congratulations to the team for an academic award, asking what the focus of practice is this week, or any number of other topics.

Don't feel like these need to be lengthy pieces. A quick text or brief email is more than enough most times.

An important thing to keep in mind here, though, is that coaches might not see your social media updates. That means you don't want to rely on that for them to stay current on what you're doing, your accomplishments, etc. Make sure you send updates to them directly, even if it's simply to point them to something on social media (as long as it's public and they can see it).

Making Your Exchanges Meaningful

Any time you engage in dialogue with a coach, no matter the platform, it's an opportunity to deepen the relationship, further your prospects for recruitment, and help prepare you for making your ultimate decision. Make sure you:

- **Ask Insightful Questions**: Coaches love getting good questions from recruits. It tells them you're really thinking about things and are taking the process seriously (believe me, there are plenty who don't). Ask about different aspects of the volleyball program and athletic department, the coach's philosophy and style, the team culture, academic support, and anything else important to you.

- **Discuss Your Fit and Contribution**: Let them know how you see yourself fitting into the program and what you believe you can contribute.

- **Express Enthusiastic, Sincere Interest**: Demonstrate your enthusiasm for both the school and the team by discussing what attracts you to it and how you envision your college experience there.

All of this revolves around continuing to do your homework about the school and the volleyball program. Keep up on current events. Reference things you heard in conversations or learned in other ways. That will help show sincere interest.

Handling Calls

As much as emails and texts can do a lot of work in the recruiting process, at some point you're probably going to end up on a call – voice or video. This is a real opportunity for the coach to get to know you, and you them. You want to take advantage of that. Here's how to do so.

1. Put it on your calendar with an alert so you don't miss it.

2. Make sure you have a suitable space with limited distractions.

3. Prepare a list of questions and things you want to talk about.

4. If it's online, access the link ahead of time to make sure it works so you can...

5. Be on time. If you're going to be late, let the coach know.

6. Have good energy. If you can't, consider postponing.

7. Answer questions honestly.

8. Ask your questions.

9. Send a follow-up email or text afterwards, thanking the coach for taking the time (you can also ask follow-up questions if you have any).

Try to relax. I know these sorts of things can be scary, especially if you haven't done anything like this before. Ultimately, it's just a conversation, though. You don't need to be anything other than yourself. In fact, trying to be someone else will probably backfire in the long run. You want to be somewhere that accepts you for you, not some other version.

Definitely have a list of questions you want answered and ask them. Recruits who don't have questions make recruiters wonder how interested they really are. And nobody is going to mind if you refer to a written list. If anything, that level of preparation is a plus.

The key thing is to be genuinely interested and engaged in the conversation. There's nothing worse than being on a call with a recruit who's showing no actual interest and whose engagement is minimal. Coaches come away from those feeling like they wasted their time and are less likely to continue recruiting those individuals.

In-person Conversations

We'll discuss campus visits in the next chapter. What I want to address here quickly are other types of in-person exchanges you might have with coaches. They could happen at a tournament, at your school, or even just randomly somewhere unexpected. Obviously, any such exchange would be subject to the rules noted in Chapter 3, so make sure you're aware of them.

Beyond that, keep in mind the things I've said earlier about making exchanges meaningful. These types of in-person ones are probably going to be shorter than a call. The key is interest and engagement. Show that you're sincerely happy to see them. Understand the situation and what it probably means for how long your interaction is likely to be. Maybe it's just a quick "Hi". Or perhaps you'll have time for a deeper exchange.

Note that if this is an informal meeting that wasn't really planned, it's probably not a good time for serious recruiting conversation. If it's something set up in advance, though, it's a different story.

Communicating with Team Members

Current members of the team can be a significant source of information about both the volleyball program and the school overall. College coaches have restrictions on instructing current student-athletes to reach out to prospective recruits. There's nothing preventing you from contacting them, however – beyond the usual social norms, of course.

Here's a list of some things you could ask a current player about:

- Team culture and dynamics

- The head coach's style and expectations

- A typical day for a student-athlete

- Balancing athletics and academics

- Team traditions and bonding activities

- Off-season schedule

- Traveling for matches

- Campus life

- Athlete housing and living situations

- Health support

Gauging Their Interest

The aspect of the process that tends to give recruits the most anxiety is trying to figure out how interested a school is in them. I should note that coaches feel the same way from their perspective. Both sides are wondering how strong the interest really is, who else the other is talking to, what the other's decision timeline is from a practical perspective, etc.

Here's how you can tell the degree to which a school is interested in you.

First, the more often you hear from them, the better. I don't mean them simply responding to you (though that's good too), but them actually initiating exchanges. And the deeper those conversations, the more interested they are. They're looking to gain a deeper understanding of you and what you might bring, while also giving you the opportunity to know more about them.

Second, the coaches show clear, specific interest in you. They don't just talk with you about general things. They're interested in specific details about you, and they remember those details in future exchanges.

Third, they watch you play a lot. I don't mean every single tournament, or anything like that. I mean, when they are at a tournament you're playing in, they don't just pop by to watch for a couple minutes. They sit and watch full sets or even matches.

Finally, they invite you for a visit. Visits take a lot of the coaches' time and effort – and budget for Official ones. They only ask those recruits they're really interested in to spend a day (or two) with the program. More on visits in the next chapter.

If you're seeing these things in your communication with a team, they're interested. That doesn't mean committed, but you're well along the path in that direction.

Communication with Multiple Schools

College coaches know you're not talking only to them. It's part of how recruiting works. You do, however, want to avoid getting yourself crossed-up and potentially hurting your relationship(s). One way to do that is to be transparent. You may get asked who else you're looking at and/or talking to. Be honest.

Another thing to do is track your different communications. That's pretty easily done with emails, and even with texts. You have the record of those exchanges (assuming you haven't deleted them) that you can refer to so you can keep things clear. Calls and anything in-person aren't so easy. For those, consider keeping a log that records dates and times, who you talked to and what you discussed.

Make it a Focus

Effective communication after the initial contact is pivotal in the college volleyball recruiting process. It's about building relationships, demonstrating your value and fit, and navigating the journey with respect, professionalism, and genuine interest. Remember, each interaction is a step toward finding the right collegiate volleyball program that aligns with your academic and athletic aspirations.

Chapter 10

Nailing the College Visit

C ollege visits are a key element of the volleyball recruiting process. It's your opportunity to see the campus, meet the team, spend time with the coaches, and get a feel for the environment you may spend four years in.

Remember that an invitation to visit campus is a strong indication that the coaches think you're someone they'd like on the team based on what they've seen and heard so far. The visit then serves two purposes from their perspective. One is to judge how well you fit. The other is to sell you on how great their school and volleyball program are.

For you, there are also two purposes. The first is to see if you can envision yourself going there (preferably for 4 years). If so, the second is to further convince the coaches (and team) that they should make you an offer. In this chapter, I'll offer my advice on getting the most out of your visits from both perspectives.

Before the Visit

As with calls, preparation is key to making the most of your visit. With that in mind, you'll want to:

- **Do More Research:** You will (hopefully) have already done at least some research on the school before arranging the visit. It's worth going deeper, though. In particular, if you know specific people you'll be meeting (per the itinerary the coaches provide), it's worth looking them up.

- **Have a List of Questions:** You'll want them covering two main areas. One is for people you'll meet on campus that you haven't met before (the team, academic advisors, strength coaches, trainers, Admissions, etc.). The other is to go deeper with the coaching staff on their coaching style, the program, the recruiting process, and the like.

- **Understand and Input on the Itinerary:** The coaching staff will put together a schedule for your visit designed to let you see a lot of stuff, meet some key people, and spend time with the team. If there are specific aspects of the campus or program you want to see, or people you'd like to speak with, ask for them to be included.

- **Be on top of the Paperwork Requirements:** You will have to submit some paperwork before going on a visit. At a minimum, that will include transcripts, and potentially test scores. If you're going to take part in any physical activity (e.g. practicing with the team, which is allowed at some levels), you'll likely need to send in evidence of a recent physical, and maybe some additional information. The coaches will let you know everything required.

Of course, you also want to make sure your travel arrangements are all in order. If it's an Official Visit, you may not have to do much more than get yourself to the airport and on the plane. If you're getting yourself to campus, though, be sure of your directions, where to park, and all those little details. It's not a good look to be late because you mistimed something or went to the wrong place.

During the Visit

Most visits will include several elements. Each of them is an opportunity for you to gain more information toward your eventual decision, as well as to solidify yourself as someone to offer a position in the team.

- **Talking with the Coaches:** You will have at least spoken with one of the coaches before, but probably not the entire staff, so this is likely to be your first chance to meet them all. Use this as an opportunity to understand their expectations and vision for the program and your potential role in it. Show your enthusiasm and ask about their philosophy, the program goals, what training is like in-season and during the off-season, etc.

- **Engagement with Current Players:** This can come in many forms. You might spend time with the team in the locker room before/after practice and/or a match. You might have one or more meals with some or all of them. They might feature on your campus tour. If you're on an Official Visit, you could spend the night with one or more of them. Use all the time you get with them to gain insights into the team dynamics, workload balance, and student life. Use your prepared questions to engage in meaningful discussions.

- **Campus Tour:** Pay attention to the facilities you'll use as a student-athlete, such as the gym, training facilities, and academic centers. Try to imagine yourself living and studying there.

- **Academic Meetings:** The coaching staff will probably set up a meeting with an academic advisor or faculty member from the department of your intended area of study. They've probably spoken to loads of prospective students before, so they'll likely have a standard spiel. Don't hesitate to ask questions, though. Understanding stuff like support services for athletes, class flexibility around training and match schedules, and opportunities for internships or research can be quite useful.

- **Attend a Practice or Game:** Coaches like to give visiting recruits the chance to observe a practice and/or match if possible. This is a major opportunity to get a sense of the team's competitive level and see the coaches in action. Make particular note of how the coaches interact with the team and how the players interact with each other.

- **Housing and Student Life:** On an Official Visit, you may spend one or more nights in a dorm. If not, you'll almost certainly at least get a tour (you should get a tour on an Unofficial Visit). Use this as an opportunity to get a sense of where you might live. Ask about dining options, campus safety, and how athletes balance social life with their responsibilities. Make sure you come away with a full understanding of any housing requirements there are for athletes and/or first-year students, and the options you'll have thereafter.

These are in one fashion formal elements of a campus visit, but they create a lot of opportunity for informal conversation. Obviously, you can use that time to get answers to your questions and to continue to show your interest in being part of that volleyball program. Don't limit yourself to that, though. Also, just have normal "getting to know each other" type conversations. These are people you may end up spending a lot of time with. It's a good idea to get a sense of who they are as individuals.

The Central Meeting

At some point on the visit – likely towards the end – you'll probably have a meeting involving the head coach focused specifically on your recruitment. This is something you want to be ready for.

They'll probably ask you your thoughts on the school and the team and see if you have questions for them after all you've seen and heard. This is obviously an opportunity for you to get further information about anything you saw or heard during the visit up to that point. It's also your chance to ask any other questions you have (e.g. prospective playing time in your first year). Use the opportunity well, especially if it might be something important to your decision-making. And if you truly can see yourself being a student-athlete at that school, this is your chance to express that.

From there, the conversation can go in several directions, depending on how your recruitment process has gone with them up to then. If you're to that point, and the coaches feel like your visit went well, you could get an offer on the spot. But that's not a guarantee, even if they intend to make you an offer.

No matter what, though, you want to walk out of that meeting understanding the timeline for things.

After the Visit

The most important thing for you to do after the visit is to reflect on it. Consider the academic and athletic fit, the campus atmosphere you experienced, and your interactions with the team and coaches. Ultimately, can you see yourself thriving there? You may feel pressure at the end of the visit to decide, but be sure to give yourself the time you need to process everything.

Of course, there are some other things you should do as well. Top of that list is sending personalized thank you notes to the people who spent time with you. Regarding the coaches, let them know your feelings after the visit. If you remain interested in the program, say so. If not, or you're not sure, be honest with them about that and any other visits or decisions you are considering.

Maximizing Your College Visit Experience

The college visit for a volleyball recruit is more than just a campus tour. It's an immersive experience that can significantly influence your decision, and you should think of it that way. Here are some additional tips to ensure you make the most of it:

- **Document your time on campus:** Take notes or keep a journal of your impressions and any important information you received. You may find these invaluable when comparing schools later.

- **Be professional and engaged:** Remember that you're evaluating them as much as, if not more than, they are evaluating you. Show interest, ask questions, and be present in each interaction, not only to make a good impression but also to collect the information and impressions you need.

- **Consider the complete picture:** College isn't just about the volleyball and academic elements. It's a total life experience. Think about your overall comfort with the campus, the city or town it's in, the people there, and whether it feels like a place you can grow.

- **Listen to your gut:** There are lots of rational aspects to picking a college. Don't be afraid to trust your instincts about the fit and potential for personal and athletic development, though.

A college visit can either affirm your interest in a program, or it can reveal it's not the right fit. Both outcomes are valuable in your decision-making. By thoroughly preparing, engaging fully during the visit, and reflecting well afterward, you'll be well-positioned to make an informed decision when that time comes.

Chapter 11

Making the Decision

The process of deciding where to play college volleyball can be as challenging as it is exciting. It involves careful consideration of both athletic and academic opportunities, along with financial implications and personal preferences.

Let's start with the offer.

The Academic Element

We should start by noting that in a lot of places, volleyball doesn't drive the bus when it comes to acceptance. Every school requires you to go through the acceptance process, of course (so don't forget to put in your application by any requisite deadline!), but that's far from a sure thing in some places. Simply meeting the NCAA requirements might not be enough.

This is particularly true of more academically rigorous schools. There might be some level of admission consideration for athletes, but not always. That means the volleyball coach can't just put you on a list and be sure you'll get in. In such places, there is often a way to get an early read on your chances of acceptance before the application window opens. The coach will guide you through that process, and any offer will be contingent on the outcome.

Understanding and Evaluating Offers

Once everything lines up, there are four types of offers you could receive from a college coach, each with its unique set of considerations:

- **Full Athletic Scholarship (aka full ride)**: This is an offer that covers tuition, housing, dining, and sometimes additional expenses like books, lab fees, and living costs. Recall what I said in Chapter 2 about the availability of these sorts of scholarships.

- **Partial Athletic Scholarship**: This type of scholarship covers a portion of your college costs and can vary from a little to a lot.

- **Walk-On Offer**: This is an offer to join the program with no athletic scholarship. Obviously, if you're talking to an NCAA Division III school or an Ivy League program where they don't have athletic scholarships, then this is the offer you'll receive.

- **Combination Offer:** This is a case where the offer is part one thing, and part another. For example, a 2-and-2 offer could be the first two years as a walk-on, then the second two years on some level of scholarship.

You may recall how I said in the discussion on creating your target list that volleyball shouldn't be the only thing you think about. Similarly, when considering offers, the size of the athletic scholarship isn't the only thing you should look at. You need to consider the full picture.

Comparing Schools and Programs

When weighing your options, be sure to include these factors in your decision-making for each school:

- **Volleyball Fit**: How well do you mesh with the team's style of play? Is the coaching philosophy one that suits you? Does the competitive level of the program fit with what you're after? Will the program help you continue to grow and develop as an athlete and move you toward your goals? Is the team dynamic one you want to be part of?

- **Academic Alignment**: Does the institution offer a program for your academic interests at the level you're looking for? Will it help you reach your longer-term aspirations? Is there meaningful support for student-athletes to succeed academically?

- **Campus Life and Environment**: Is the campus culture and community one where you feel you belong and can thrive? Does the location, size, and student population fit with what you're after? How do you feel about the housing options, both when you first get there and in future years?

- **Financial Considerations**: Beyond any athletic scholarship, what is the school offering by way of non-loan financial assistance, like academic scholarships and any available grants? Is this assistance reasonably renewable from year to year (e.g. you just need to keep your grades up)? Are there any additional costs you might have to attend this school compared to others you're considering (like living in a dorm vs. living at home)? Ultimately, what's it going to cost? Remember that traveling between home and campus is part of your college costs.

Don't be afraid to ask lots of questions at this point. College coaches and individuals in Admissions, Financial Aid, and all other departments at the school expect this. Gather all the information you need to make a fully informed decision. And involve anyone you think can advise you.

Also, don't think that the offer you get is necessarily the final offer, unless they tell you so. You might be able to leverage the fact that you have interest from multiple schools (assuming you do) to get a better offer. Regarding athletic scholarship, that would involve talking with the coach. If it's regarding academic or other kind of institutional aid, that would be a discussion with Admissions and/or Financial Aid (remembering that coaches usually can't have anything to do with that).

It's a good idea to let coaches and schools know about the offers you're getting elsewhere. Sometimes the simple fact that you're getting them is enough to get you an improved offer.

Decision Timelines

There are several factors that can influence the decision timeline a college coach gives you when making an offer. They include:

- **Early Decision/Early Action**: Some schools have early decision or early action admissions, usually in the first semester. There are often incentives for going this route, so it's worth understanding.

- **Rolling vs. Non-Rolling Admissions:** Some schools accept and decide on applications at any time. This is rolling admissions. Others have certain timelines for when applications must be in, even outside of early action/early decision.

- **Academic program deadlines**: At some schools, there are deadlines for applying to specific academic programs.

- **National Signing Day**: The official period to sign a National Letter of Intent (NLI) starts in November of the year before you plan to attend college. You don't *have* to sign then, but there might be pressure to do so.

Alongside these influences, there are several factors that can come into play regarding a coach setting a decision deadline. How far out you are from potentially joining the team is one, as coaches will want to move more quickly the closer they get. How much they want you is another consideration. If they really want you, they'll be more flexible.

The other big factor is who else they're looking at. If, for example, it's between you and another recruit they see as being largely of equal value, they're likely to ask you to make a quicker decision than might otherwise be the case.

See it from their perspective. They'll be thinking about how long they might be able to keep the other recruit on the hook. The worst-case scenario for them is that you ultimately reject their offer and while they were waiting for you, the other recruit accepted an offer elsewhere, leaving them with nothing. Always keep in mind that college coaches are deciding among different options just like you are.

Communicating Your Decision

Once you've made your decision, these are the steps you should take:

1. **Notify the Chosen Program**: Contact the coach of the school you're committing to as your first step. Express your enthusiasm and gratitude for the opportunity and ask them for the next steps.

2. **Inform Other Programs**: Next, out of respect, inform coaches of other programs with whom you've been in

serious communication. Be direct and honest.

3. **Let Your Coaches/School/Club Know**: If they don't know already, having been part of the process, inform your current coaches about your decision, as well as your school and your club (if applicable).

4. **Update Your Recruiting Profile**: If you're using an online recruiting profile and/or University Athlete, update it to reflect that you're now committed. This will avoid having schools reaching out.

5. **Public Announcements:** While not required, you may wish to announce your commitment publicly through social media, etc. This is an opportunity to share your excitement, and to say thanks to those who've supported you along the way.

Make sure you do #1 and #2 as your first two things. Don't let college coaches you've developed a relationship with find out from social media, or through the grapevine, that you've committed. How you handle this will influence the impression you leave on these coaches, and you never know if that impression will come into play in the future.

After Your Commitment

Post-decision, the focus shifts to preparing for the transition to college athletics. There are a number of potential next steps, depending on the school and when you make your commitment. In the immediate term, that might include things like putting in your application and filling out Financial Aid paperwork. Later on, there will be things like sending in your sizes for gear, submitting medical info for the trainers, giving bio material to Sports Info, and a bunch of other onboarding.

Regardless of when you make your commitment, though, there are a few things you should stay focused on:

- **Engage with Your Future Program**: Stay in regular contact with your future coaches and teammates. Attend any team events or meetings that are open to you. Get to know any of the other commits who will be your fellow incoming classmates. Use current team members as a resource to help you in the transition and stay connected with everyone. That will help make your first days on campus a lot smoother.

- **Stay on top of the Academics**: Make sure you continue working toward graduation and that you fulfill any entrance requirements for your chosen institution. And ensure you meet the NCAA's academic requirements if that's applicable.

- **Athletic Development**: Continue your development as a volleyball player and an athlete. The coaches can let you know what they'd like to see you work on, and they might share with you the sort of workout program the team is on. Keep them updated on your play, including your competitive schedule if you have one. Don't give them any reason to question their decision by slacking off, just going through the motions, having a poor attitude, or anything like that.

The coaches will certainly want to stay engaged with you along the way. If you've picked the right program, the players will as well. Don't put all the work on them, though. There are times of year when they're dealing with a lot of other things – like during season. If you have heard nothing in a while, it's fine to shoot them a text or drop them an email. They'll appreciate it and will help build stronger relationships ahead of you getting there.

Part II

Specific situations and FAQs

Chapter 12

Considering NIL in Volleyball Recruiting

T he introduction of Name, Image, and Likeness (NIL) rights for student-athletes altered the landscape of college athletics in a major way. NIL rights empower student-athletes to monetize their personal brand through endorsements, sponsorships, social media, personal appearances, and more. This isn't the place to talk about building your personal brand and all of that, but I can at least share with you how NIL can affect recruiting and how it might work for you.

Laws, Rules, and Regulations

The NIL landscape remains a patchwork of state law, conference/school policy, and NCAA guidance. The NCAA continues to distinguish permissible NIL from impermissible pay-for-play and other prohibited arrangements, but the enforcement landscape has been shaped by ongoing litigation – particularly around recruiting-related NIL restrictions – and by the growing role of third parties (including collectives). In Division I, the post-House framework also adds more standardized reporting and review expectations for certain third-party NIL deals.

The practical takeaway is that you should treat NIL rules as local: know the athlete's state law, the school's NIL policy, and the conference's expectations, and ask the compliance office how they handle collective involvement and NIL reporting. Don't assume what's permissible (or enforceable) at one school will be the same at another.

NIL for Internationals

Please note that there are some significant restrictions on student-athletes attending school on a student visa receiving NIL money. The US laws around employment of those on such visas require that anything considered employment – and this includes NIL deals – closely relates to their field of study. Before agreeing to any deals, you would need to consult with the school's international students' office to make sure you don't put your visa at risk.

NIL's Influence on Recruiting

As with everything in the recruiting process, keep in mind that there are two sets of considerations – yours and the school's. I'm sure you can think about what those are for you. Help grow your following. Link you with potential sponsors. Stuff like that. What's in it for them, though?

For sure, coaches think first about what a recruit brings from a volleyball perspective. That doesn't mean they don't also think about the off-court elements, though, especially when deciding between similar athletes. As much as going to the right school can help boost your own NIL prospects, bringing in someone with a good brand can raise a program's profile. That attracts better recruits, more donations, etc.

I'll give you an example. When I coached at Radford University, we had a couple of team members with large social media followings. Without us really doing anything, that helped us land recruits. Those recruits told us so!

So, while thinking about what's in it for you, make sure you're also framing things with regard to what's in it for them.

What to Look For

What exactly should you look for from an NIL perspective when considering a school to target, or when deciding between programs?

- **NIL Policies**: Make sure you research and understand a prospective school's NIL policy. Don't assume that if you know one, you know them all.

- **Program Attractiveness**: You can leverage programs with strong support more than those with little support. Broadly speaking, schools in larger markets and/or with larger social media followings offer more lucrative NIL possibilities and better opportunities to grow your platform. That said, highly engaged smaller communities can also provide valuable partnership options.

- **Available Resources**: A school that offers education and resources for exploring and managing NIL opportunities – to include legal and financial aspects – will help you go further.

- **Other Athletes' NIL**: The sorts of NIL activities other athletes at that school are involved in could influence its attractiveness. It's probably a good sign if multiple athletes are well situated. Too much competition in your niche could be problematic, though.

- **The Volleyball Team**: Consider how a program's approach to NIL aligns with your values and how it might influence team dynamics. A culture that supports all players in pursuing NIL opportunities, regardless of their role on the team, can be beneficial.

- **Balance**: Maintaining your focus on volleyball performance and academic achievements will be vital. Look for schools that emphasize balance and support student-athletes' holistic development.

As the NIL landscape continues to evolve, its impact on volleyball recruiting will probably grow. For recruits, understanding and leveraging NIL can enhance not only the college experience but also future career opportunities.

Chapter 13

Transferring: 4-year to 4-year

The introduction of the Transfer Portal by the NCAA definitely affected the college sports landscape in major ways. It's not unlike free agency in professional sports. Athletes dissatisfied with their current situation can use the Portal to seek a change. This sort of thing was always possible. The Portal just made it easier.

NCAA transfer restrictions have generally become less limiting than they once were. In many situations, athletes can transfer and be eligible right away – especially when they leave their previous school in good standing academically and meet progress-toward-degree requirements at the new school. The details still evolve and can be case-specific, so treat any transfer decision as a compliance conversation first, as your school's compliance staff can tell you what applies to your exact situation.

Just because you can doesn't necessarily mean you should, though. Let's look at both sides of the subject.

Reasons to consider transferring

There are some perfectly valid reasons to seek a transfer. They include:

- **Academic:** The current institution doesn't offer the desired major, or the academic quality in the chosen field of study is lacking.

- **Athletic:** Limited long-term opportunity for playing time or a coaching style that doesn't align with the athlete's development goals.

- **Coaching Change:** A new coaching staff with different philosophies or strategies that don't align with the athlete's strengths or aspirations.

- **Cultural Fit:** The school's environment, team dynamics, or campus culture may not be a good fit for the student-athlete's personal values or needs.

- **Financial:** Changes in scholarship status, unforeseen financial hardships, etc.

- **Geographical:** Desire to be closer to home because of family circumstances, health issues, or personal commitments.

- **Personal Growth:** Seeking new challenges or opportunities that are not available at the current institution.

Avoiding at least some reasons above is possible with a bit more research and/or consideration before making a college selection, as discussed in Chapter 5. Things can change which necessitate a transfer, though. That's why the system has mechanisms in place to facilitate it.

That said, there are also not so good reasons to transfer, such as

- **Impatience for Playing Time:** Expecting immediate playing time rather than being patient and earning the opportunity.

- **Conflict Avoidance:** Leaving because of minor conflicts with coaches or teammates instead of addressing and re-solving the issues.

- **Chasing Prestige:** Transferring to a higher-profile pro-gram for the sake of prestige alone, without considering fit or development opportunities.

- **Peer Influence:** Deciding based on where friends are go-ing or transferring without fully considering individual needs and goals.

- **One Bad Season:** Reacting impulsively to a challenging season without considering the potential for growth in the current program.

- **Perceived Lack of Attention:** Feeling undervalued or seeking more recognition without realizing the value of team roles and contributions.

- **Impulsive Decisions Based on Emotions:** Making a hasty decision during a moment of frustration or disappointment.

Players who transfer for these sorts of reasons tend to just bring their own personal issues along with them. As a result, going to a new school rarely solves the problem. So really think about things before you commit yourself. And be prepared to defend your reasoning, because you will definitely get asked when you talk to new schools.

Consider your Credits

Definitely look at what could happen with your credits and academic standing if you transfer to a new school. This is less of an issue for student-athletes in their first or second year of college. Most of the classes in those first couple years transfer without too much issue, albeit they may only go through as credits rather than the specific courses.

It's once you're in your major that things can get really challenging. Transferring as a Junior in your third year could cost you quite a bit, potentially forcing you to have to do an extra year at the new school. Make sure this is something you factor into your thought process as you ponder a transfer.

The Mechanics of Transferring

As I noted, it's relatively easy to transfer now. If you're at an NCAA school, you simply go to your Compliance Officer and tell them you'd like to enter the Portal. If you're in Division III, you alternatively can simply do a self-release by filling out a form. Of course, if you're thinking of going from a non-NCAA school to the NCAA, or to another non-NCAA one, there is no Portal.

Regardless of Portal/non-Portal, ultimately you should think of transferring very much like the initial recruiting process. You want to reach out to schools that you think would be a good fit and let them know you're in the Portal, if that's the mechanism for you. Then you go through the communication, visits, etc. similarly to your initial recruiting process.

Yes, coaches can see everyone who enters the Portal. Just as it's not good enough to simply create a recruiting profile and wait for people to come to you, though, you can't expect that just because you entered the Portal that coaches will start beating down your door. The Portal is quite thin on details, so there's no real way for you to stand out. It takes coaches some work trying to gather information. Better for you to put yourself directly in front of them rather than hoping they pick you out of the crowd. Plus, coaches outside the NCAA – which might be a viable option – won't see you there anyway.

No guarantees

It's important to understand that just because you enter the Portal – or otherwise put yourself out there to transfer - it doesn't mean you'll automatically get picked up by a new, better program. The NCAA's Transfer Portal Trends dashboards (updated annually) are a useful reality check because they show what actually happened to athletes who entered the Portal in the most recent reported cohort.

The most recent indoor volleyball figures (women's – no men's data listed) indicate that only 60% of Division I athletes who entered the Portal in 2024 enrolled at a new NCAA institution, 6% withdrew from the Portal (likely meaning they stayed at their current school), and the remaining 34% will still listed as active in the Portal. Within that group, 82% stayed in Division I, while most of the remainder ended up in Division II.

Among undergraduates on athletic scholarship, 58% received a scholarship at their new school (though no indication of whether that was full or partial), while 18% did not, and 24% failed to successfully transfer to a new NCAA school (still listed as Active in the Portal). Out of those not on scholarship who entered the Portal, 46% failed to find a new NCAA program, 29% transferred without going on scholarship at their new school, while only 25% were able to secure a scholarship by transferring.

The figures for Beach Volleyball (all listed under Division I) are similar.

In Division II, the numbers are much worse at just 34% of Portal entries landing at a new NCAA school. About 2/3rds who did successfully make a move went to another Division II program, while 26% managed a move to Division I. Only 28% of undergraduates who entered the Portal having been on scholarship successfully found themselves a new scholarship situation, and only 14% of those who didn't have a scholarship to begin with found one for themselves.

I should note that just because the NCAA doesn't show someone as having moved on to another NCAA institution, it doesn't mean they didn't transfer. They could have moved on to another type of school (NAIA, NJCAA, etc.), where they may or may not have received a scholarship. Or they may have stopped playing. The NCAA just doesn't have that information to report.

It's important that you're aware of these figures because we tend to only hear about the successful transfers. Nobody reports about the student-athletes who went into the Portal and couldn't find a new place to play.

You probably can't change your mind

One of the big reasons athletes who go into the Portal don't end up on an NCAA roster the next season is their current school has moved on. There's no place for them any longer.

Sometimes, there's bad blood. The athlete says or does things around going into the Portal (or says nothing!) that leaves the coaches angry, frustrated, disappointed, etc. Any trust there is now broken. It's hard to get that back.

Even when there isn't bad blood, coaches have to think about the good of the program. If you tell them you plan on leaving, they plan on you not being there anymore. They recruit someone new. And if you're on a scholarship, they give it to someone else. You can't expect them to renege on any agreement they made just because you change your mind.

There goes your scholarship

Another factor in all this is that you could lose your scholarship if you enter the Portal. Different coaches and schools have different policies here. The NCAA allows them to pull it, though. So if you put in for a transfer after the Fall season, and plan on staying through Spring term, you might find yourself with a tuition bill.

Just trying to be real

I know the last few sections of this chapter were pretty negative about transferring. That wasn't done to scare people with legitimate reasons to seek a transfer from doing so. It was done, however, to prevent unrealistic expectations. I've spoken with athletes whose attitude about their initial recruitment was to anticipate transferring after their first year. And I've seen international athletes who treat college volleyball like a professional sport where they look for a better contract each year. It's not that simple and the odds aren't strongly in your favor.

Chapter 14

Transferring: 2-year to 4-year

I f you start your college playing career at a JUCO, at some point you'll look at transferring to a 4-year school to continue your education. In some ways, the process is very similar to the one I described in the last chapter. You want to treat it the same way you treat your initial college recruitment. Identify target schools, reach out, etc.

That said, there are some elements of this process you should know as you think ahead.

Permission to Contact

Be aware that the NJCAA requires student-athletes to get permission from their current school before they can officially talk to other institutions. Student-athletes often formalize this process through a "Permission to Contact" letter or form. The current school's athletic department or coach must grant this. The specific rules and procedures can vary by conference and school, though, so you'll want to consult your current coach or athletic director. There isn't a similar requirement among CCCAA schools, but it's always a good idea to talk to your coach and/or administration before initiating the transfer process.

It's easier if you graduate

Everything in the 2-to-4 transfer process is easier if you have/will graduate from your JUCO. That avoids any academic eligibility issues and means there are no constraints on communication with 4-year college coaches, especially after your second JUCO season. It also means not burning bridges with your JUCO coaching staff, who could be quite useful for you in the transfer recruiting process (see below).

If you don't graduate

For one or more of the reasons I outlined in the last chapter, you may opt to transfer from your JUCO after a single season. In that case, depending on your circumstances, going to another JUCO might be the best option.

If, however, you want to pursue a transfer to a 4-year school after just a single season – or after two when you won't be graduating – be aware that both the NCAA and NAIA have restrictions. This especially applies to student-athletes who did not meet the criteria as a Qualifier (see Chapter 3) when they graduated from high school. Worst-case scenario, you sit out a year before becoming eligible at the new school.

Leveraging your JUCO coaching staff

Broadly speaking, people see JUCOs as steppingstones to 4-year colleges and universities. The JUCOs understand this at an institutional level, so they have structures in place to help students move along.

This is especially true with coaches. They know most of their athletes are looking to use their program to make themselves recruiting prospects for 4-year schools. As such, they see helping their players take that next step as a core part of their job. And the better they do, the more attractive they become to future recruits looking for that same steppingstone. In other words, it helps make their program stronger and more competitive.

The more experienced the JUCO coach, the more players they've seen go on to play at the next level. That gives them a wealth of insight and loads of contacts. You want to capitalize on that by listening to their guidance on suitable targets for you and how to go about pursuing them. Seek any help they can give you. It could pay off handsomely.

Chapter 15

Recruiting for non-US volleyball players

E verything I've presented in this book up to now applies to both US and non-US athletes going through the recruiting process. In this chapter, though, I want to address how things are different for those trying to come to the US to play college volleyball.

It's easier to recruit domestically

The first thing I should say here is that it's almost always easier for coaches to target domestic athletes than international ones. Seeing international recruits compete in-person is harder (though it can happen). The Admissions process is more complicated for internationals. Even just getting on a call is tougher with non-domestic recruits given time zone differences and the like.

What all this means is that an international recruit needs to bring something more to that program than what they're likely to get from domestic recruits. Mainly I'm talking about level of play here, but there are other elements such as diversity of experience that a coach might judge to be a valuable addition. Either way you look at it, though, most coaches will only recruit international players they see as being able to contribute to the program fairly quickly.

You should look at this two ways. It might mean you get a lot of playing time your first year, which you may see as an excellent thing (no guarantee, of course). At the same time, though, it may mean you need to pick your targets a little differently. For example, you might benefit more from approaching slightly less successful programs than you would in other cases. They, after all, are more likely to see you as someone they could use right away.

Eligibility and Amateurism

NIL has changed what athletes can earn while in college, but international recruits still need to clear the NCAA's eligibility certification process – especially around what they did before full-time collegiate enrollment. There isn't a single simplistic rule. It's the full set of facts: teams/leagues played for, any agreements or contracts signed, and what money or benefits (if any) were received beyond actual and necessary expenses.

Don't rely on hearsay about which leagues "count" as professional. If you're aiming for the NCAA, assume the Eligibility Center (and the school's compliance office) will want documentation and will make a case-specific determination. The safest approach is to disclose everything early and let the certification process tell you what, if anything, needs to be addressed.

The NAIA is largely in line with the NCAA, but has some differences.

Finances and Your Budget

In Chapter 2, I talked about how scholarships work at US colleges. There is a tendency for international recruits to think entirely about full athletic scholarships. While this is understandable, given the costs involved, it's best to take a broader view. Unless you're truly an elite level athlete, restricting yourself to only those schools willing and able to offer you a full athletic scholarship will prevent you from seeing some potentially quite strong opportunities.

You should know that most schools offer at least some kind of academic scholarship for applicants with a good academic record. The size of those scholarships varies considerably, however, so I can't tell you what you'd get. Schools also offer a variety of grants and other sources of funding that you may be able to access. Therefore, it's worth taking a more comprehensive view than just one tied to the athletic scholarship.

Let me provide an example from my own experience. When I coached at Radford University, our full annual cost of attendance was about $36,000. We were not fully funded, so the best we could do for athletic scholarships was about $30,000 if it was a high caliber recruit. That left a gap of $6,000. A recruit with sufficiently good grades, however, could see this gap filled by an academic scholarship. We in Athletics had no influence on those scholarship decisions, so we couldn't promise a recruit we'd cover their full cost of attendance. That was a real possibility, though, if they were willing to go through the Admissions process.

The best approach is to have a budget figure when you connect with college coaches. That's the amount you could afford to pay toward your college costs. There's a good chance any coach you reach out to will ask, assuming you don't share it with them up-front. And if you work through one of the agencies or services that tries to help get international players recruited to the US, they will get the question on your behalf.

So have a budget figure in mind that works for you and be flexible about how a school might get to that number.

Don't fixate on the volleyball

In the chapter on developing your target list of schools, I shared a lot of different factors that go into deciding where you want to go for college. Most of it has nothing to do with volleyball, or even athletics more broadly. It's about the environment you'll be in. This is key.

Make sure you don't just pick a school based on volleyball!

There are too many stories about international athletes who come to the US to play their sport in college – volleyball or otherwise – who quickly become disillusioned. Why? Usually because they got so focused on the sport that they forgot to consider everything else.

I once talked to a Polish setter who was looking to transfer to a new school after a single year. He confessed to me he didn't research things nearly enough. The location, in particular, was really frustrating for him. This is something that he might have avoided by digging more into the school and its geography.

One of the real challenges is doing campus visits. They are often more difficult in terms of time and money than is the case for US recruits. That makes research all that much more important for international recruits.

Men vs. Women in Recruiting

There are something like 8 women's college volleyball teams to every men's team – and there's currently no men's Beach college volleyball (at least outside of club). As I noted in Chapter 2, scholarships for the men – at least in Division I – could grow considerably. This is great news, but the reality is this only covers a couple dozen schools. That means full athletic scholarships for the men, which have been extremely rare up to now, are likely to become more common, but still will be few in total number compared to the women. In other words, men's college volleyball recruiting for a foreign athlete is more challenging, especially if you're looking for a scholarship. There are numerous international players on men's college rosters, so it's far from impossible. There are simply fewer opportunities.

Definitely consider a JUCO

In Chapter 2, I mentioned 2-year colleges (JUCOs) and outlined how they can be good options for many people for several reasons. In some ways, this applies even more so to international recruits. A lot of internationals take the JUCO path to gain entry into the US college system. Many of them have lots of scholarship money. And where they don't, often the costs are a lot lower than for a 4-year school at a comparable level. Plus, the level of play can be quite good! So if you're not getting the response you'd like from 4-year schools, consider the JUCOs. See Chapter 14 to learn more about transferring from a 2-year to a 4-year college.

Chapter 16

Options outside the US

Very few countries have a collegiate sports system like the one in the US. In most parts of the world, if you want to be both a student and an athlete, you'd have to do them separately. You'd attend a university and play for a local club team. Adult club volleyball is a much bigger thing in many places than it is in the States, making that a readily available option.

That said, there are two countries with systems somewhat similar to the one in the US in that you can play for a school-affiliated team.

Canada

The Canadian system shares a lot of similarities to the US system in terms of competition structure, the setup of individual programs, etc. It is significantly smaller, however. It also doesn't have the same level of resources, nor the same level of media exposure and fan support, especially compared to the upper end of the NCAA system.

Notably, the Canadian system lacks the US amateurism requirement. They will accept players who previously played professionally. Also, you can play up to 5 years there compared to 4 years in
the US. There are athletic scholarships, but they tend to be less
than what some US schools can offer.

United Kingdom

The collegiate sports structure in the UK is quite different from
that in either the US or Canada. It is based on a club model similar
to what I discussed regarding US college club volleyball in Chapter
2. The members mainly run these clubs, and they primarily recruit through open-gym ("taster") sessions and potentially trials
for teams that compete in the UK university system, known as
BUCS (British Universities and Colleges Sport). Some clubs have
coaches. Others do not. Many only practice 1-2 times/week.

There are, however, some of what are referred to as performance
programs. These programs have a structure that closely resem-
bles college programs in North America. They have direct university funding, with coaches and additional support in the areas of
strength training and athlete well-being. They train several times
per week, and they even have scholarships to a greater or lesser
extent, depending on the university. Not surprisingly, they compete in the upper echelons of BUCS.

These performance programs do recruit internationally. That
tends to be more often for graduates from North American col-

leges who have used up their eligibility. They sometimes take undergraduates as well, though, if the fit is right.

I should note that college players in the UK can take part in multiple competitions. Alongside BUCS, they often play in the National Volleyball League (NVL) and/or regional leagues in their area. And players can be part of multiple teams, just not in the same competition. For example, when I coached at the University of Exeter, our teams played in the South West regional league alongside BUCS, and some players separately played for local club teams in the National League.

Recruitment

If you're interested in playing for either a Canadian university or one of the performance programs in the UK (which currently are all in England), the process is like the one in the US. Do some research, find the coach's contact info and reach out. There will be some differences in the actual processes, but the key elements outlined in this book will serve you well, regardless.

If, on the other hand, you're happy with the lesser commitment of playing club volleyball, then it's all about getting in touch with someone from that club. They'll be able to tell you how to get involved.

Chapter 17

FAQs

In this chapter, I will address some of the common questions that come up in the recruiting process.

Should I use a recruiting service?

The biggest value for most people in using a recruiting service is time savings. They can be extremely useful in the research process to help you create your target list of schools. And also in initiating and organizing communication. If you're potentially looking at a wide range of schools, the tools these services offer can save you a lot of time and effort. If you've got a fairly narrow list, though, maybe not so much.

Of course, there's also the option of letting a service essentially act like your agent. By that I mean they actively work on your behalf, reaching out to college coaches, helping you with your materials, offering advice, and whatever else they can to land you in the right situation. Naturally, the more they do for you, the higher the cost.

Ultimately, there's a time/effort savings and potential added benefits vs. costs decision to make. That's going to be different for each family, so I can't tell you whether you should go that route.

Two things to keep in mind in your thinking, though. First, using a recruiting service is no guarantee. Second, you still have to be the one communicating with coaches, going on visits, etc. They are recruiting you, not the service, after all.

Is it worth going to college camps?

The answer to this question is it depends what you're after. If you just want to have a pleasant experience and learn some things, then go for it! However, if your primary goal is to get recruited, I believe it is important to proceed with caution.

The fact of the matter is that most college camps are primarily money making events. That's the simple reality. They are neither designed nor intended to function mainly as recruiting mechanisms, especially in Division I and II. In fact, the NCAA does a lot to discourage that kind of set-up.

Don't get me wrong. Camps can still be useful in your recruitment strategy. They're an opportunity to spend time on a college campus, interact with college coaches and players, and increase your overall understanding of things. If a school you're actually having good communication with is running a camp, and it makes sense for you to attend financially and timing-wise, then going can certainly give you a lot of useful insights into that school and volleyball program. I just wouldn't view them as a showcase. Easy to waste a lot of money that way.

Are showcases worth doing?

Again, it depends. If the idea is just "to be seen", then I have strong reservations. That can work, but only if the event attracts coaches from the kinds of schools you're targeting. Otherwise they're just taking your money.

If, on the other hand, you've been doing your research, reaching out to schools, and all that, and want to give them an opportunity to see you perform in-person, then it could be quite useful – especially if they may not get another good opportunity (for example, you don't play club or your club isn't playing at the bigger events). Again, you'll want to go to a showcase that's likely to get attendance from coaches at the school(s) you're targeting.

Can I get recruited if I only play in high school?

Absolutely!

There's no doubt that the process is easier if you play Juniors club. College coaches prefer those tournaments because they can see a bunch of potential recruits in one place. Recruiting budgets aren't unlimited, after all. The process, however, is the same. It will just probably rely more on video than being seen in-person.

How important is the club I play for if I play Juniors?

Not as important as some people might have you believe.

I think people considerably overstate the idea that you need to be "seen" by playing in major tournaments and/or playing Open. Coaches aren't wandering from court to court at tournaments hoping to randomly come across the next impact player for their program (it happens, but very infrequently). They go to events with a list already in-hand (which is why you reach out). You can't rely on them spotting you by chance just because you're playing Open at the XYZ National Qualifier.

That said, clubs can definitely be useful in the recruiting process. Some have recruiting coordinators who do a good job of promoting their players and otherwise support them in finding a school (just be cautious of anyone promising a scholarship). Experienced club coaches can be very helpful in targeting the right level of college volleyball for you. They can also be good referrals. It's worth asking around to hear what people have to say – especially recent club alumni.

Above everything, though, you want to be part of a club and team that's going to challenge you to be better and help you grow as a player. This is particularly true in the younger ages (let's say 15 and below) where not much recruiting is happening anyway.

What if I'm looking to be a multi-sport athlete?

I'm going to start by telling you straight up that being a multi-sport athlete in Division I and Division II is extremely difficult. It happens on rare occasions, usually involving sports in opposite seasons, but coaches generally aren't big fans. Keep in mind that there is significant off-season work at this level.

Things are very different in Division III. There, it's much easier to do multiple sports because the permissible off-season work is very limited. I've seen many dual-sport athletes, and even some tri-sport ones.

Obviously, trying to get recruited to play multiple sports is much more complex than for just one. For that reason, pick your priority sport for your main recruiting thrust. Then you can narrow your target list based on those where playing your other sport(s) is doable. Be very open and honest about your intentions in your communication with coaches.

Can someone recruit me to play both Beach and Indoor?

The answer to this depends on the school. Some have Indoor players on their Beach team (or vice versa). Others don't. In a lot of ways, you can think of it very similar to being a multi-sport athlete.

Keep in mind that the NCAA doesn't allow student-athletes on a Beach scholarship to play on the Indoor team. The other way around is fine, though.

Is Beach recruiting different from Indoor?

Not really, no. The process is the same. Naturally, there are some timing differences related to when the Beach season runs, but everything I've shared in this book applies to both.

Is Men's recruiting different than Women's?

As with Beach vs. Indoor, there are some timing differences, and it's been my experience that decisions happen later on the Men's side. Beyond that, though, the process is the process.

What if I am injured during the recruiting process?

If it's a relatively minor injury, like an ankle sprain that keeps you out for a couple of weeks, I wouldn't worry too much. Yes, it can be upsetting if it happens right before some key tournament or other event where you intended to showcase yourself. If you're doing your work sharing videos and connecting with coaches, though, this will be a minor bump in the road.

A major injury is obviously a more challenging situation. Honestly, some coaches won't want the uncertainty that brings to the equation, and will opt to turn their attention elsewhere. That might involve pulling an offer they've made. Others will take a different view. How a coach reacts often depends on their expectations of you when you join the team. If they see you as an immediate impact player, and that's specifically what they're looking to bring in, the risk of them moving on is higher than if you're someone they see as more developing over your career.

Of course, timing and recovery timeline factor into the equation. Regardless, make sure you communicate openly and honestly about the injury. How you handle the situation could influence the way college coaches see you, and by extension, how they see you fitting in the program and with their plans for it.

What is "Red-Shirting"?

The term "red-shirting" refers to when a player sits out a season, thereby not using one of their seasons of eligibility (remember, in the NCAA you generally have 5 years to play 4 seasons). Most often we hear about red-shirting because of a significant injury. This is known as a medical red shirt.

There are times, though, when a player sits out for other reasons. For example, a coach may see a lot of potential in a new recruit, but doesn't feel they will get playing time as a first year. In a case like this, rather than the player use up a year of eligibility, the coach and player may decide to red-shirt that season. The player would still practice and do all the other team activities. They just wouldn't play.

If you're in a potential red shirt situation, make sure you know the current NCAA rules on the subject. Generally speaking, if you've played less than a certain fraction of your team's matches that season, you can successfully apply for a red shirt (known as a medical waiver). The timing of when those matches took place matters, though.

Chapter 18

Bonus Chapter: Using AI to help in the Recruiting Process

S eeing as we now live in a time where AI tools exist to help us do innumerable things, it's worth addressing how they could apply to the college recruiting process. Because the tools and their capabilities change all the time, I'm going to avoid getting too specific here. I can at least help you think in some broad ways about how you can use them as you go about your recruitment efforts.

Keeping on top of recruiting rules and timelines

It's always useful to know about key upcoming dates on the recruiting calendar. You can, of course, do a standard search on "NCAA recruiting calendar" or something like that. Using AI, however, is likely to be quicker. Here's a sample prompt you could use:

> *I am a [insert your graduation year] high school graduate look-ing to be recruited to play college volleyball. What are the key recruiting calendar dates I should know regarding NCAA recruiting rules around contacts, visits, etc. that apply to me over the next 6-12 months?*

You can also use AI to keep you updated on changes in NCAA rules and policies. Here's an example:

What key developments have there been in the last 6 months re-lated to the NCAA, particularly regarding the rules for student-ath-letes?

Naturally, you can make that more specific if you want to focus more narrowly. There are often developments in the NIL arena, in particular, that may be worth keeping tabs on.

The point is, you can use AI to help you stay updated on key timelines in your recruiting process and on any developments that might affect your recruitment and/or future life as a student-ath-lete.

School and team research

The first notable area AI can help with is researching and targeting the right colleges. AI tools in this context can process information from college websites, databases, forums, etc. to help come up with your list of schools.

Start by inputting specific criteria important to you. This is the stuff we talked about in Chapter 5. The more detailed your input, the more tailored the AI's output will be. Here's a sample prompt:

> *Provide a list of colleges with NCAA Division II volleyball programs that offer a business management degree, in the northeastern United States, with a campus size of less than 10,000 students.*

Using your criteria, an AI tool can scan through college data, identifying institutions matching your preferences. It can compare programs across a variety of dimensions. If you like rankings, maybe ask it to use a scoring system based on metrics like athletic fit, academic quality, and social environment and assign a score to each school so you can rank them.

Once you have a shortlist, you can use AI to dive deeper into each college. For instance, you might ask the AI to gather detailed information about the volleyball team's win-loss record over the past five years, its notable alumni, or the employment rate of graduates from the business management program. Here's a sample prompt for that:

> *Summarize recent volleyball team achievements and post-graduation employment rates for business management students at XYZ College.*

As you continue through the recruiting process, you can use AI to keep updated by receiving ongoing insights about your targeted schools. That can give you lots of stuff to talk about in your communications with those schools, as well as help you eventually make your decision.

Communications with schools

There are potentially several ways AI tools can help make the communication part of the recruiting process easier and/or more effective. Since this is the most time-intensive part of it all for most recruits, it's well worth exploring your options and looking at what AI can do for you.

The most basic aspect of this is writing emails for you. It's pretty simple to get AI to use the research it already did for you to craft an introduction email. Here's a sample prompt for that:

Using the information from my AI-driven research on [School Name]'s volleyball program, and incorporating my personal athletic profile and achievements, generate an introduction email to Coach [Coach's Name]. Here are the details to include:

- *Personal Introduction: My name is [Your Full Name], I am currently a [Your Grade] at [Your High School] in [City, State], and I play as a [Your Position] on for [High School Team Name or Club Team Name].*

- *Program Interest: Mention my keen interest in [School Name]'s volleyball program because of their [mention specific attributes of the program].*

- *Alignment with Team's Needs: Highlight how my playing style and strengths as a [Your Position] align with the team's known strategic preferences and current roster gaps. Emphasize my skills in [mention specific skills], which match the team's style of play, particularly noted in games against [mention any specific game or team they played recently].*

- *Academic Alignment: State my intention to major in [Your Intended Major] and my interest in [School Name]'s [mention specific academic facilities or programs], demonstrating my dual focus on athletics and academics.*

- *Recent Achievements: Briefly list my top athletic achievements, such as [mention any recent tournaments won, awards received, or leadership roles], which reflect my capability and potential as a recruit.*

- *Call to Action: Suggest setting up a meeting or a phone call to discuss my potential fit with the team, or invite the coach to view my next game or review my online highlight reel at [Link to Highlight Reel].*

- *Closing Remarks: Conclude with an expression of enthusiasm about the potential to contribute to and grow with [School Name]'s volleyball program, thanking the coach for considering my application.*

Please format the email with a professional tone, ensure grammatical accuracy, and organize the content logically for clear communication.

Obviously, you can adapt that basic framework to suit. In fact, you can even ask AI to create a prompt for you specific to your situation!

While AI tools can be super helpful in writing emails and things like that, I must issue a word of caution. If your communication with the schools you're targeting comes off as fake or a simple form letter, it will not help you. Probably the opposite. So make sure you don't give the impression of just sending the same thing to every school.

Here are some other ways AI can help in the communication aspect of the recruiting process:

- **Automated Scheduling and Reminders:** This is useful for sending periodic updates and/or following up after initial contacts or visits. AI can also send reminders, ensuring you don't miss something important.

- **Personalized Communication Templates:** AI can analyze communication from college coaches to generate personalized response templates that maintain your voice while addressing the coaches' messages.

- **Writing Enhancement and Proofreading:** AI writing tools can help ensure that your communications present you professionally. Before sending an important email to a coach, run the content through an AI-based proofreading tool to check for any spelling, grammar, or stylistic errors.

- **Sentiment Analysis:** AI tools equipped with sentiment analysis can evaluate the tone and intent of communications received from college coaches and provide insights into a coach's level of interest.

- **Monitoring and Analyzing Communication Patterns:** This data can help you judge when it's best to reach out to maximize the prospect for a prompt response to your email or text.

- **Predictive Analysis:** Some AI tools can analyze your communication history with each program to predict which are most likely to offer you, helping you focus on the most promising opportunities.

No doubt, there are other potential uses for AI tools not covered here. Maybe you should ask one, "What can AI tools do to help me in my college volleyball recruiting process?" and see what ideas come up.

As I said at the beginning, I'm not providing specific tool recommendations here because the landscape is always changing. A quick search on YouTube will provide you loads of videos offering tips and advice on the latest tools and how to use them. If you want to at least explore using AI in your recruiting, definitely do some research to figure out what tool or tools best fit with what you're aiming to achieve. It could end up saving you much time and effort.

Just don't hand everything over to AI, though. Ultimately, recruiting is about finding the right match for you. AI can only ever be an assistant. You're the one that needs to make the final decision.

Chapter 19

Conclusion – Embrace the Journey

T he path to becoming a collegiate volleyball player is full of challenges, decisions, and milestones. Each chapter of this book has aimed to equip you with the knowledge, strategies, and insights needed to navigate this complex process with confidence and clarity.

The recruiting landscape is ever-evolving, influenced by changes in regulations, technological advancements, and shifts in the sports culture itself. Yet, the core principles of hard work, perseverance, and strategic planning remain constant. By mastering the art of communication, leveraging your social media platforms, and making informed decisions, you're setting a sound foundation for your future in college volleyball and beyond.

Remember, the recruiting process is not just about securing a spot on a college team. It's about finding the right fit for your academic, athletic, and personal growth. The effort you put into researching schools, engaging with coaches, and showcasing your abilities is an investment in your future. It's important to approach each step with an open mind, resilience in the face of setbacks, and a commitment to your goals.

To the student-athletes - This journey is an opportunity to showcase your passion for volleyball, your dedication to your craft, and your readiness for the challenges of collegiate athletics.

To the parents, coaches, and mentors - Your support, guidance, and encouragement are invaluable to these athletes as they pursue their dreams.

As you move forward, carry with you the lessons learned, the relationships built, and the experiences gained throughout the recruiting process. Whether it's celebrating your commitment to a college team, adapting to changes along the way, or persevering through uncertainties, remember that your journey is uniquely yours. Embrace it with enthusiasm and pride.

The world of college volleyball offers incredible opportunities for growth, competition, and camaraderie. As you transition from a recruit to a student-athlete, continue to strive for excellence, both in class and on court. The skills and values you develop during this time will serve you well beyond your collegiate career, in volleyball and in life.

Thank you for allowing me to be a part of your journey. Here's to the next chapter of your volleyball career, filled with success, learning, and unforgettable moments.

Please leave a review

Dear Reader,

Thank you for choosing *The College Volleyball Recruiting Playbook: Strategies for Success*. I hope this book proves a valuable asset in your journey to play college volleyball.

Would you consider taking a few moments to share your thoughts for other readers? Reviews help prospective future readers in their decision-making process. Books with more reviews tend to get more attention as well. I want this book to help as many players and families as possible as they navigate the college recruiting process. You can be part of that by visiting the site where you bought this book – or perhaps your favorite book review site (e.g. Goodreads) – and posting a review.

Of course I'd love it if you post a review on social media or whatever platform you have (blog, podcast, etc.). If I see it, I'll share it!

All the best,

John Forman

About the Author

J ohn Forman is the developer of the well respected volleyball coaching education blog at CoachingVB.com. He started it in 2013 as a resource for coaches in England where he lived and coached at the time. It quickly garnered global readership, however. These days it receives hundreds of thousands of visitors each year.

John's coaching experience includes NCAA Divisions I, II, and III, Junior College, and Juniors levels in the US. In the UK, he's coached at the university and National Leagues levels. John also coached a professional team in Sweden. He's spent time with teams and programs from Juniors all the way up to to the national team level in Argentina, England, Germany, Hungary, Italy, the Netherlands, Poland, Portugal, Spain, and Switzerland.

One of John's major side projects is Volleyball Coaching Wizards, which he's developed with partners Mark Lebedew and Lauren Bertolacci. Together they've interviewed dozens of highly successful coaches from around the world, and at a variety of levels of play. From those interviews they've published multiple books.

John is a member of the American Volleyball Coaches Association (AVCA), holds a CAP III certification from USA Volleyball, and is a Volleyball England Level 3 coach. He earned a PhD from the University of Exeter (UK), an MBA from the University of Maryland, and a BS from the University of Rhode Island.

Also by John Forman

In support of his coaching blog, in early 2024, John authored *The Perfect Drill*, a guide to designing maximally effective volleyball drills and games. You can get your copy from CoachingVB.com or find it on your favorite book store at https://books2read.com/ThePerfectDrill.

And as part of his work on the Volleyball Coaching Wizards project, John has also co-authored three books, one of which has been translated into Spanish. You can find them at http://volleyball coachingwizards.com/books, or in your favorite online retailer's store.